Calgary's Best Bike Rides and Trails

Calgary's Best Bike Rides and Trails

Lori Beattie

FIFTH
HOUSE

Cover and interior design by Articulate Eye
Cover illustrations by Brian Smith / Articulate Eye
Photographs © 2004 Lori Beattie
Edited by Meaghan Craven
Copyedited by Ann Sullivan
Proofread by Alex Frazer-Harrison
Scans by St. Solo Computer Graphics

The publisher gratefully acknowledges the support of The Canada Council for the Arts and the Department of Canadian Heritage.

 Canada Council **Conseil des Arts**
for the Arts **du Canada**

We acknowledge the financial support of the Government of Canada through the Book Publishing Industry Development Program for our publishing activities.

Printed in Canada by Friesens

02 / 2008

First published in the United States in 2004 by
Fitzhenry & Whiteside
121 Harvard Avenue, Suite 2
Allston, MA 02134

National Library of Canada Cataloguing in Publication Data

Beattie, Lori

    Calgary's best bike rides and trails / Lori Beattie.

Includes index.

ISBN 978-1894004-91-6

    1. Bicycle touring—Alberta—Calgary—Guidebooks. 2. Calgary

(Alta.) —Guidebooks. I. Title.

GV1046.C32C24 2004   796.6'4'09712338   C2004-900529-4

Fifth House Ltd.
A Fitzhenry & Whiteside Company
1511, 1800-4 St. SW
Calgary, Alberta T2S 2S5

1-800-387-9776
www.fitzhenry.ca

Contents

Acknowledgements

Thanks a million to my husband, Keith Dewing, who coasted and climbed many of the routes in this book. Thanks to my son, Oscar Dewing, who helped me test all aspects of the kid-friendly routes as he trailed behind in the bike trailer. All the playground and ice cream stops have been thoroughly researched because of Oscar. Thanks to my friends Lisa Woodward, and Carmen, Randall, and Graham Berlin, who headed out with map in hand to test many of the routes in this book.

My publishing experience has been very enjoyable and professional thanks to Liesbeth Leatherbarrow, Charlene Dobmeier, Simone Lee, and Cathy Bogusky at Fifth House Publishers. Thanks to my editors Meaghan Craven and Ann Sullivan, and proofreader Alex Frazer-Harrison, who helped me produce a quality product. Thanks also to Mike McCoy and Brian Smith of Articulate Eye Design, who spent many hours on the layout and design of this book.

Thanks to all my Fit Frog hiker pals, who made sacrifices to test all the coffee shops in this book and who gave me ideas for interesting bike routes. And a huge thank you to my mum and dad, Marg and Don Beattie, in Woodstock, New Brunswick, for instilling in me the love of self-propelled outdoor activity.

Introduction

In my first book, *Calgary's Best Hikes and Walks*, I led you by foot through Calgary's unique neighbourhoods, along forested pathways, from panoramic viewpoints to comfy cafés. In *Calgary's Best Bike Rides and Trails* you'll travel farther, on brand new routes that combine smooth pathway pedalling with dips and climbs on hilly side streets and occasional rides on bumpy dirt paths through wilderness parks.

Biking in Calgary is a great way to stay healthy and fit while finding the hidden gems that can only be seen when you get off the main roads. The variety of routes in this book offers something for everyone. Families can travel the kid-friendly routes that stick to the paved paths and quiet streets. Fit cyclists, who want to move more quickly, can cycle the lesser-known paved paths in the north and east, or head out for a full day on the Tour de Calgary figure eight pathway ride. Leisurely cyclists can enjoy a meandering ride through Confederation Park or a sunset glide along the Glenmore Reservoir pathway. Gardening enthusiasts can take notes on the home and garden routes that host character homes and colourful yards. Nature lovers leave the city behind on peaceful rides along the open plateau of Nose Hill Park in the far north or through wildflower meadows in the east end of Fish Creek Provincial Park, in Calgary's south end. Accompanying all of these routes are suggestions for snack breaks and shopping detours. Take a break at one of the interesting, independently owned lunch, ice cream, or coffee shops along the trail, where you can fuel up en route or enjoy a post-pedal cool-down with a hot coffee and a homemade meal.

Where will you go on your first outing? Plan a family ride with the baby in a bike carrier and the kids by your side. Travel the quiet streets of Bowness to the halfway stop at Bowness Park. Playgrounds, a summer water park, minigolf, and lots of water for rock throwing make this the perfect place to take a break.

For your second ride of the season, head out on the Wildwood to Bridgeland route. The variety in terrain presents lots of physical challenges, while the changing scenery keeps your mind occupied. The warm-up along the Bow River Pathway prepares you for the climb to Renfrew, where Rocky Mountain and downtown Calgary views are your reward. Descend into Bridgeland, a neighbourhood with pop-bottle-coloured stucco bungalows, manicured yards, and tree-lined streets. It's smooth sailing along the Bow River Pathway all the way to Edworthy Park, followed by a steady climb to the quiet streets of Wildwood.

Later in the season, when your legs are well tuned, try one of the long routes. What a treat to be able to cycle non-stop for five hours through a city of nearly a million people. A combination of paved pathways and quiet streets means avid cyclists can pick up the pace and work up a sweat. You don't need to leave the city to feel refreshed and fit.

Depending on the season, you can bike in Calgary after work when the sun shines late or early on a crisp fall morning when the sunrise warms the sky. It's convenient, fresh, and fun. Explore the city on two wheels and have a self-propelled adventure in your own backyard!

1

Gear and Clothing

Before heading off to the bike shops and outdoor stores with credit card in hand, it's a good idea to determine your needs as a cyclist. A recreational rider who plans to explore the city during the summer months has different gear needs than a rider who is keen to ride year-round for pleasure and commuting. The one piece of gear all cyclists need, however, is a bike. The best bike is the one you already own. It does not need to be fancy, and in fact, the less attractive the better: you won't have to worry about someone stealing it. Bikes last a long time and require very simple maintenance to keep them running safely, so chances are your old bike will be just fine for urban outings. Once you've taken your bike out of storage, take it to a reputable bike shop for a tune-up.

Buying a New Bike

If you don't already own a bike, go to one of the many reputable outdoor stores or specialty bike shops in Calgary. Their sales representatives will be able to tell you about the latest and greatest in bike technology. The following is a primer on the kinds of bikes you will find in Calgary bike shops.

CALGARY BIKE SHOPS
This is a sample of Calgary's established bike shops.

South Calgary
The Bike Shop: 801–11 Avenue SW (265-0735)

Mission Cycle: 2310–4 Street SW (228-3598)

Single Track Cycle: 1503–15 Avenue SW (244-2464)

Spokes & Attire: 735–10 Avenue SW (283-1523)

Sport Swap: 701–11 Avenue SW (261-8026) or 6999–11 Street SE (253-5184)

The Cyclepath: 9176 Macleod Trail South (250-7717)

Mountain Equipment Co-op: 830–10 Avenue SW (269-2420)

North Calgary
Ridley's Cycle: 223–10 Street NW (283-1421)

Lifesport: 1110 Gladstone Road NW (270-4501)

Vitasport Cycles: 3007 Centre Street North (276-5115)

Sport Swap: 3320–20 Avenue NE (280-4877)

Bow Cycle & Sports: 6531 Bowness Road NW (288-5422)

The Cyclepath: 10, 2015–32 Avenue NE (250-5654)

Road bikes have skinny tires, low-slung handlebars, and narrow saddles that are designed to reduce chafing on long rides. They are fast and easy to pedal on pavement, but they're not much good off-road. These bikes are the most efficient choice for experienced cyclists who prefer long rides on the road.

Mountain bikes have wide tires that work well on a variety of terrain types. They have many gears, which allow the rider to manage hill climbs efficiently by gearing down for the climb. The forward riding posture is great for steep hill descents on single-track dirt trails, but it is not necessary for urban cycling. In fact, many people find this forward posture uncomfortable. If you choose to buy a mountain bike, make sure it fits you well. That way, you'll avoid developing the sore wrists, neck, and back that come from riding in the forward posture on an ill-fitting bike.

Hybrid or *cross* bikes are almost as fast and easy to pedal as road bikes, while being almost as versatile as a mountain bike. These bikes allow their riders to sit upright and have a wide range of gears, making them a popular choice for commuters. I rode a hybrid bike when testing all the routes in this book and found it suitable.

Comfort bikes are essentially mountain bikes with smoother tires and a few more comfort-oriented features such as riser handlebars that allow you to sit in an upright position, and a wide, cushy saddle. Comfort bikes are great for short rides on flat terrain.

Cruisers have up to three speeds, big saddles, and they allow the rider to sit upright. They are perfect for biking at a relaxed pace through neighbourhoods, but are not the best choice for hilly routes or outings longer than twenty kilometres.

Recumbent bikes sit low to the ground and are quite comfortable because of their bucket seat, which lets the rider sit in a laid-back, relaxed position. They are more aerodynamic than upright bikes and can move much more quickly. However, because their riders sit so low to the ground, recumbent bicycles present visibility problems. Recumbent riders must also develop a set of specialized skills to operate their bikes at maximum efficiency.

Back in the Saddle

For those who do not cycle throughout the winter, the first bike ride in the spring can be a painful experience. You can expect a bit of rear-end discomfort initially, but if your bike saddle (seat) is the proper size and height, and in the right position for you, biking should not be painful. The following is a brief overview of what to look for when choosing a new saddle, or how to adjust your current one.

The Height

If your seat is too low, you will bend your knees too much and put unnecessary pressure on them, as well as increase pressure on your buttocks. Fix this right away by increasing the seat height until your leg is almost extended when the pedal is at its lowest point. This new position may feel strange at first, but it is the most efficient and comfortable position for riding. You'll know the seat is too high if you rock from side to side on your saddle when you pedal.

The Tilt

The angle of the saddle should be relatively horizontal. Some men prefer the front to be slightly higher than the rear, and some women prefer the front slightly lower than the rear, but avoid extreme angles as they can cause discomfort.

HANDLEBARS: NECK, SHOULDER, BACK, AND HAND PAIN

A proper reach to the handlebars is the key to enjoying a comfortable bike ride. If your handlebars are too close or too far away from your body, you may experience neck, shoulder, back, and hand pain. You may have to move forward and backward on your seat throughout your ride if your reach to the handlebars is too short or too long. To change the length of your reach, you usually have to replace the handlebar stem. If your reach is correct, you should be able to comfortably bend your elbows and keep a straight back while riding, and there should be equal pressure on your hands and seat. If you think your reach is wrong, head to a reputable bike store to assess the position of your handlebars and buy the right stem for you.

BIKING WITH KIDS

When planning a Calgary ride with your children, remember that kids are not motivated by how fit they're becoming, how much weight they're losing, or how fast they're going. The only thing that matters to kids is having fun!

Bikes, Trailers, or Trail-a-bikes?

Children over the age of nine should be able to handle their own bikes. Infants who cannot hold their heads up cannot wear helmets and therefore should not be transported by bike. Infants over the age of eight months can hold up their heads, wear helmets, and safely ride in bike trailers. Some brands of bike trailers come with special infant seats that provide lateral support so they won't tip over on bumpy roads. Rear bike seats that attach to an adult bike are another option for transporting children. Bike trailers are safer than bike seats because if you fall, your baby won't fall with you. In addition, a bike trailer allows you to carry gear, snacks, and toys. However, bike trailers are low to the ground and may not be visible to distracted motorists, even when you install a safety flag.

Many bike shops stock Calgary-made Chariot Carriers (www.chariotcarriers.com). Mountain Equipment Co-op also sells its own bike trailer, which is much less expensive than most other brands. If your child is too big to sit in a trailer but too young to ride his or her own bike, consider purchasing a trail-a-bike. This is a small bike without a front wheel that attaches to your bike and trails behind.

Snacks and Stops

Healthy food options are great, but don't forget to pack some trail treats as well. Bring a lot of snacks, and plan on stopping to play often so your children's energy levels stay high. See Chapter Three for a variety of smart snack recipes that will appeal to kids, and adults too!

Get Fit

Before heading out for the Tour de Calgary ride, make sure you first try a few short routes. All family members are at risk of injury if you set out on a route that doesn't match your family's level of fitness and endurance.

Stay Safe

Have all of your family's helmets fitted at an outdoor store or cycling shop, and ensure that everyone wears a helmet at all times on the road. Infant helmets for children in bike trailers are available at Canadian Tire. Ride single file, use your bell, and announce "bikes on the left" when passing. Follow the rules of the road and make sure your children practise safe biking before hitting the trails. The Can-Bike Skills program, developed by the Canadian Cycling Association, is currently the only nationally recognized bike education program. The program focuses on developing the skills and knowledge necessary to operate a bike in a wide range of traffic and weather conditions.

Learn-to-Ride Courses: Can-Bike courses are offered by the Elbow Valley Cycling Club. The 20 hour "Cycling Sense" program enables the graduate to choose an appropriate bicycle, adjust it for proper fit, and perform basic maintenance. It also offers participants instruction in correct riding procedures, handling techniques, and group riding skills. Contact information: 283-2453, www.elbowvalleycc.org

Kids Bike Safety Programs: Safety and education programs for kids are offered through the Calgary Safety Council. Location: #108, 2116–27 Avenue NE, Stockman Centre; contact information: 287-2990; www.calgarysafetycouncil.com

The Size

There are many bike seats on the market designed for a variety of body types. Men's saddles are narrow while women's are wider to accommodate the female hip bones. Most bikes come with saddles built for men.

The Fit

Your sit bones should rest on the back of the saddle. If your saddle is too narrow, your sit bones will hang over the edge. If this happens, the soft flesh between those bones will take all the pressure. Ouch! A saddle that is too wide, however, can chafe the inside of your thighs as you ride.

WOMEN'S SADDLE SIZES

If you have the wrong saddle size, riding a bicycle can be painful. When the position of your sit bones (ischial tuberosities) does not fit your saddle, you will experience discomfort. This is often the case for women, whose sit bones are wider than men's. Saddles made specifically for women are also wider, providing space for both sit bones to rest on the saddle instead of one side slipping off the edge and causing discomfort. The length of a woman's saddle is also usually shorter to minimize painful private-part pressure.

TRANSPORTING BIKES

Sometimes you will need to transport your bike to the start of a route, making a bike rack necessary. Bike racks fit all styles of vehicles. Choose between trailer-hitch-mounted racks; racks that easily fit on the car trunk and hold up to four bikes; hatchback racks; roof racks that keep bikes upright; or racks that fit over a spare tire.

Safety Considerations and Gear

Make sure you are prepared for falls or collisions with cars when cycling or rollerblading on the streets and pathways of Calgary. The most basic and essential safety item for bikers and skaters is a properly fitted helmet. Helmets must be less than five years old, have no dents, and must never have been left in a hot car for days on end. They must fit well and sit properly on your head to be effective..

Helmets

If you don't wear a helmet while biking, a simple topple on pavement could lead to serious brain damage. A bike helmet consists of a shell and a polystyrene core. The core of a bike helmet contains its life-saving property: expanded polystyrene (EPS), a foam product that absorbs the force of an impact. After absorbing the force of just one impact, the EPS is useless and must be replaced. If you can see a dent or scuff mark on the shell of your helmet, throw it away. EPS also dries out and hardens over time, making it less shock absorbent, so replace your helmet if it is more than three years old.

When buying a new helmet, make sure its impact absorption capabilities are certified. A variety of governing bodies have set impact standards for bike helmets. Look for a CSA, ASTM, CPSC, or Snell B90/B95 certification sticker before buying any bike helmet. And make sure your new helmet fits properly!

Helmets fit much better today than they did even a few years ago. If your helmet does not fit you perfectly, buy a new one. Have the helmet fitted at the store so you know what it feels like when the helmet sits correctly on your head and the straps are working properly. If you can answer yes to the following questions, your helmet is a good fit.

- Flat—Does the helmet sit flat on your head so that your forehead is covered?
- Tight—Is the helmet tight enough that (even without the chinstrap connected) it won't fall off if you shake your head and bend forward?
- Touch—Does the top of your head touch the top of the helmet?
- Strap—Are the straps adjusted to prevent the helmet from moving should you fall?
- Flick Test—Once the straps are connected, flick the front of the helmet upward. Does the helmet barely budge forward or backward?

Once you have a perfectly fitted helmet, take care of it. To keep your new helmet in working order, make sure you store it properly. Keep it away from hot places, such as a sealed car on a hot day. High temperatures can melt and shrink the shell, soften the glue, or bake and harden the EPS foam and reduce its shock absorption capacity.

Visibility Gear and Other Safety Accessories

Even if you never plan to ride at dusk or in the dark, it is best to be prepared for it. A light could make the difference between being seen by a car or being hit by it. If portions of your ride take you through unlit areas, such as a shortcut through the local park, you might even consider getting a powerful off-road headlight. A bell and mirrors are other must-have safety accessories for urban bikers.

By law in Calgary, you must have a bell on your bicycle, so save yourself a ticket and warn those pedestrians that you are approaching. A mirror is another helpful piece of equipment, especially if you plan to ride on roads, but you will not be penalized for not having one. Using a mirror while riding takes a bit of getting used to: half of what you see in your mirror is yourself.

> **REFLECTIVE VESTS**
>
> If you plan to be anywhere near road traffic, a reflective vest is a good—and cheap—investment. Designed to be worn over your jacket, a reflective vest will improve your chances of being seen in traffic. Bright orange with bright yellow reflective stripes, a vest makes a wonderful safety backup if you are caught out when dusk descends. Get one at Mountain Equipment Co-op, 830–10 Avenue SW.

Clothing

Specialized outdoor clothing is made with fabrics that keep you warm when it's cold; keep you dry when it's wet; and breathe, so that your sweat doesn't soak you. Although you can go cycling in a pair of jeans and a T-shirt, there are clothes that will make your ride more comfortable when Mother Nature changes her mind and the snow starts to fall on that warm May day.

Cycling Shorts

Specially designed Lycra® cycling shorts have sewn-in padding that is called chamois (pronounced "shammy"). The chamois layer in the shorts covers the inside seams, protecting your body from chafing. If you're not interested in the wind-resistant benefits of Lycra®, or if modesty steers you away from skin-tight fabrics, get a pair of loose-fitting cycling shorts with a built-in mesh or Lycra® inner chamois, or wear a pair of shorts over a pair of Lycra®-chamois cycling shorts. Lycra®-chamois shorts are essential for cycling comfort at the start of the season and on rides that last more than thirty minutes.

FEATURES OF SPECIALIZED CYCLING CLOTHING

Cycling clothing does not need to be complicated and technical. Its purpose is to make your cycling outings more comfortable. The following are some design features to look for in cycling clothes.

"Breathability"

Cycling can be a sweaty activity, especially if you have a hill or two to climb along the route. All clothing designed for cycling is made from lightweight polyester-blend fabrics that "breathe," or allow vapour from sweat to escape rather than condense.

Differential Cut

Cycling jackets and tops are cut longer in the back so that they cover the small of your back when you are in a crouched riding position. Many of them also feature pockets on the back for storing a snack, a water bottle, or a wallet.

Longer Sleeves

When you extend your arms to reach the handlebars on your bike, your shirtsleeves tend to ride up. Cycling tops have longer sleeves than those of typical T-shirts, so your arms are always covered.

Reflectivity and Visibility

The more visible you are to cars and other pathway users, the less likely you are to get into an accident. Many cycling clothes are designed with reflective stripes and piping. If you don't want to buy a new jacket, simply purchase adhesive reflective stripes to stick on your bike and your clothing.

Gloves

Cycling gloves have padded palms designed to absorb road vibrations when you're riding and prevent road rash if you fall. Try an open-fingered glove in the warmer months. When the thermometer drops, you'll appreciate the insulated, lobster-style gloves that group the first two and last two fingers for extra warmth. These gloves allow riders to use their fingers for braking and gear switching.

Cycling Glasses

Chinook winds that kick up all sorts of dusty debris, and Calgary's trademark sunny, blue-sky days are a couple of reasons to carry glasses with you on a ride. Glasses keep the wind, dust, bugs, low branches, and ultraviolet radiation out of your eyes. Make sure the cycling sunglasses you choose allow air to flow between the glasses and your face. Sunglasses that hug the face may fog up when you start to perspire. It is also important to choose glasses made of impact- and shatter-resistant plastic.

Dressing for Outdoor Activity

The best way to stay warm or to cool off when biking is to layer your clothes. This allows you to remove a layer for a hill climb or add a layer post-climb, when your heart rate drops or the wind starts to blow.

The wicking layer is your first layer, your underwear layer. It comes in direct contact with your skin and is responsible for moving moisture away from it. Wicking layers should be made of synthetic materials designed to let moisture pass through. Cotton underwear will trap moisture and chill you. Synthetic materials disperse perspiration so you remain warm even when you are damp.

The insulating layer is your second layer—and possibly third or fourth, if it is very cold. It traps and reflects heat back toward your body. Except on a hot summer day, avoid cotton as an insulating layer. When cotton gets wet, it stays wet, and on cool days it can chill a sweaty cyclist. The insulating layer should "breathe" so moisture can move through the layers, away from the wicking layer and your body. Fleece, some of which is made from recycled pop bottles, is environmentally friendly and is the best insulating fabric. Its structure—millions of fibres and air pockets—traps warm air molecules, keeping you warm even when the fleece is wet. It also dries very fast. Wool is also a fine insulating layer, but it doesn't dry as quickly as fleece does and it becomes quite heavy when wet.

The shell layer is the final outer layer that protects your body against wind, rain, and hail. When buying a shell layer, decide when you'll use it the most. The nice thing about cycling in Calgary is that, most of the time, you are close to cover if the weather turns miserable. If you want to be able to ride in the rain in relative comfort, it's a good idea to take along a shell when you cycle. If you are buying a new jacket for your urban outings, you will find three choices: lightweight windproof/water-resistant shells, waterproof jackets, and waterproof/breathable jackets.

Windproof/water-resistant jackets are light shells that protect riders from wind and light drizzle, and pack down to a small, easy-to-carry bundle. Such jackets are less expensive than waterproof/breathable jackets, and they provide adequate cover from the elements when your outing is less than a couple of hours long and thunderstorms are not in the forecast. These jackets breathe, but they will not protect you from a downpour.

Waterproof rubbery rain outfits do not "breathe." If you are sweating under such a jacket, your sweat will eventually soak you. A rain jacket of this type with pit zips (zippers under the armpits) will allow some ventilation. These jackets are a cheap option for casual cyclists who do not plan to ride in the rain very often.

Waterproof/breathable jackets are expensive but are made from materials that effectively stop rain from getting in and allow vapour from perspiration to escape. Gore-Tex® is a well known brand name, but many other materials, such as Entrant®, Extreme®, Hydroflex®, and Ultrex®, are also waterproof and breathe. Gore-Tex® is made of Teflon sandwiched between polyester or nylon fabrics of varying weights. The Teflon in the Gore-Tex® has holes that are small enough to keep water droplets out, but big enough to let water vapour from sweat escape. The fabrics used in this class of jacket can be heavy and stiff for rock climbers who need a durable outer layer, or light and flexible for runners and cyclists. The downside to these jackets is that they are heavier, less breathable, and more expensive than wind shells. The upside is that they offer the best protection from the elements.

Bags

The urban cycle routes in this book can take half an hour or a full day. It is nice to be able to take a few items with you, no matter the length of the route, just in case hunger creeps up and you need a snack, or a storm rolls in and you need a jacket. A backpack will work when your load is light or for short rides, but bags that fit on your bike are more comfortable to carry. The bag options below start small and get big enough to take you and your gear across Canada.

Handlebar bags are my bag of choice for urban outings. They attach directly to your handlebars and are big enough for a camera, lunch, and an extra jacket. Get the one with the rainproof map holder on top so you can see your city route as your ride.

Under-seat bags are small-capacity bags that attach under your saddle. These are great for key storage, a small repair kit, snack, or wallet.

Rack trunks attach to the shelf of your bike rack. Sleek and roomy, they offer moderate storage capacity without much wind resistance.

Courier bags sling over your shoulder and are perfect for commuters who carry important documents to work.

Panniers are roomy, rack-mounted bags that keep heavy loads low and centred on your wheels. Panniers are usually sold in pairs and are designed for either front or rear racks. Some models are versatile and will work on either the front or back.

BIKE REPAIR AND MAINTENANCE

The great thing about urban cycling is that you are never far from help when you need it. If you plan to cycle farther afield, it may be time to learn how to repair your bike. Tires can spring leaks and chains can break. Bring a small repair kit on long rides so that you can continue cycling even if your bike breaks down. A typical bike repair kit includes an Allen key, tire iron, spare inner tube, and patch kit. Learn how to maintain your bike and make simple repairs by taking a course on bike maintenance offered at a local bike shop or through the University of Calgary Outdoor Program Centre (220-5038) or Canada Olympic Park (247-5412 or 247-5452).

2

Fitness for the Trails

Cycling is a wonderful activity that the whole family can enjoy. If you are not used to physical activity or if you are planning to hit the trails after winter hibernation, make sure you start slowly with some flat, easy routes. The foundation of cardiovascular fitness you will achieve when biking in the city will allow you to tackle more demanding, longer outings with strength and confidence. This chapter addresses the basics of cardiovascular fitness and provides tips on how to cycle safely and effectively.

Aerobic and Anaerobic Exercise

Oxygen plays an important role in providing energy. Understanding how your body uses oxygen during exercise will help you to better enjoy your cycling excursions. The terms aerobic and anaerobic refer to whether or not oxygen is involved in creating energy for your body while exercising. Moderately intense activities that are repetitive and of prolonged duration, such as cycling on flat terrain, hiking, swimming, snowshoeing, and jogging, are aerobic: your body consumes oxygen when performing these activities. Intense activities of short duration, such as a steep, quick hill climb on a bike, or sprinting, are usually anaerobic: your muscles operate without the benefit of oxygen. Such activities leave you breathless.

Aerobic and anaerobic conditioning are complementary. Aerobic conditioning prepares the body for activities of a longer duration, and anaerobic training increases the body's ability to climb steep hills on a bike more efficiently. While biking, you'll use a combination of these two conditioning types as you pace for pleasure on flats and climb for oxygen on hills. It is important to understand when you body needs to slow down so that you reduce the intensity of the ride.

Heart Smart Cycling

If you are starting to exercise after a period of inactivity, use the "talk test" to measure how hard you are working. If you can inhale enough air to talk comfortably while exercising, you are working at about fifty to seventy percent of your maximum heart rate. SLOW DOWN if you cannot talk. You should never feel dizzy or nauseated while performing any physical activity. Following are three steps that help you to assess your present level of fitness and increase it.

Step 1: Determine Your Maximum Heart Rate

You can use your heart rate, measured in beats per minute, to evaluate the intensity of your activity. Calculate your maximum heart rate—the maximum number of times your heart contracts in one minute—to discover your optimum training intensity. For people over forty who are starting an exercise program of moderate to high intensity, and for people who have a history of heart problems, the safest way to calculate maximum heart rate is by having a doctor-monitored stress test. For others, a commonly used formula for calculating maximum heart rate is to subtract your age from 220. If you are thirty years old, your maximum heart rate is 190 beats per minute.

Step 2: Choose an Appropriate Level of Activity (Training Heart Rate)

Once you have determined your maximum heart rate, you can estimate an optimum training heart rate using the following calculations:

For low fitness level: maximum heart rate multiplied by 60%

For average fitness level: maximum heart rate multiplied by 75%

For athlete: maximum heart rate multiplied by 90%

It is safe to start an exercise program at 60% of your maximum heart rate. If you want more specific training guidelines, with defined benefits, refer to the zone ratings described in the following table:

ZONE	ZONE NAME	% OF MAXIMUM HEART RATE	BENEFIT
1	Low intensity and weight control	50–60%	A good zone for beginners to build their cardiovascular foundation and burn fat. Activities such as pedalling at a leisurely pace, walking, and swimming keep your heart rate in this zone.
2	Weight control and aerobic	60–70%	Burns lots of fat and maintains basic fitness level. Endurance activities that keep a consistent pace and are aerobic fit into this zone. Try biking a 15–30 km route that combines flats and hills.
3	Aerobic	70–80%	Improves cardiovascular strength. You feel out of breath but your muscles do not burn in this zone. Biking up hills, jogging, or adding sprints to your swimming routine take you into this zone.
4	Anaerobic	80–90%	Interval training (adding short bursts of speed to an activity) improves your muscular endurance for future physical pursuits. Activities that make your muscles burn and leave you gasping for air fit into this zone. Try a fast hill climb on your bike or gear down and pedal hard on the flats.
5	Insanity	90–100%	The zone name says it all!

Step 3: Monitor Your Fitness Progress (Resting Heart Rate)

As your level of fitness increases, your resting heart rate decreases. Knowing your resting heart rate is a good way to monitor your fitness progress. Take your resting heart rate before you get out of bed in the morning or when you are relaxed. To measure your heart rate, hold the palm of your left hand facing upward and place two or three fingers your left wrist. Find your pulse and count the beats for fifteen seconds. Multiply this number by four to get your heart rate in beats per minute. You can also use this technique to measure your heart rate while exercising.

Warming Up and Cooling Down: Training Tips for Cyclists

Warm Up for the Ride

Don't climb that hill at the start of your ride! Your heart and all your muscles need a chance to warm up in order to work efficiently. If you notice you cannot catch your breath when you start biking, slow down and pedal easy for the first ten minutes. Your muscles are not replete with oxygen at the beginning of an activity and need time to warm up; start slowly and breathe deeply during your warm-up so that your muscles can fill with oxygen, then make the big push uphill. A relaxed transition from anaerobic to aerobic activity makes for pleasant pedalling and keeps you injury-free throughout your ride. Post-pedal stretches and a proper cool-down will also help you to stay limber and avoid injury.

Cool-Down Stretches

When you have completed your bike route, consider doing some cool-down stretches. The following stretches are designed to lengthen muscles and move joints through a full range of motion. Stretch when your body is warm and focus on maintaining a neutral body alignment in order to avoid injury.

Ideal body alignment brings the ear over the shoulder, the shoulder over the centre of the hip joint, and the hip joint over the knee and ankle joints. This posture is called neutral alignment. Throughout your day, whether you are sitting, walking, or lifting, try to maintain a neutral spine. It is especially important to have neutral alignment when you are stretching.

Calf and Achilles Tendon Stretch

The technique: Place both hands on a vertical surface, such as the trunk of a tree, the back of a bench, or the side of a picnic table. With hands shoulder width apart, keep one leg forward with the knee bent and the other leg extended straight back. Both feet should be pointing forward. Feel the stretch in the back of the straight, extended leg, below the knee. Now bend this leg until you feel the stretch in your Achilles tendon, which connects the heel with the calf muscles. Switch legs and repeat.

The benefit: Maintains flexibility in the calf muscles; helps prevent Achilles tendon tightness and plantar fasciitis (a sharp pain felt on the bottom of the heel when weight is placed on the foot). Plantar fasciitis is an inflammation of the plantar fascia, a band of tissue on the bottom of the foot, and can become chronic if not treated.

Quadriceps Stretch

The technique: Stand on one foot with your knee slightly bent. Lift the heel of the other foot toward your back. Use your hand, a towel, a bench, or a picnic table to hold your elevated leg in place. Make sure you maintain a neutral spine alignment (do not arch your back) and keep your knees very close to each other. Switch legs and repeat.

The benefit: Stretches the quadriceps, the large muscles at the front of the thigh, and helps prevent knee and back problems.

Hip Flexor Stretch

The technique: Kneel on the ground on one knee. Bend your other leg in front of you, with the foot flat on the ground. The kneeling leg should be slightly extended, with your knee positioned just behind your buttocks. When you shift weight onto your front leg, the stretch should deepen in your hip flexors, at the top of your thigh. Be careful not to let your front knee go too far forward over your toes. Avoid knee strain by moving your front foot forward. Maintain a neutral spine throughout. Do not arch your back. Repeat stretch on the other side.

The benefit: Stretches the hip flexors, which extend from the front of the hip to the lower back and are used to bring the leg forward when walking. When you sit, the hip flexors are shortened. Too much sitting leads to short or tight hip flexors, which can pull your body out of alignment and hyperextend your back, leading to lower back pain.

Hamstrings Stretch

The technique: While standing, lift one leg in front of you onto a bench or picnic table seat. With your heel on the bench, point your toes toward the sky. Maintain a neutral spine as you bend forward at the hips with arms extended forward. Feel a pull in the back of the leg between your buttocks and your knee. Repeat stretch on the other side.

The benefit: Tight hamstrings (the muscles at the back of the thigh) can lead to lower back problems.

Gluteus (Buttock) Stretch

The technique: In a standing position, bend your right leg and place your right ankle on a bench, picnic table, or on your left knee. The higher the object the more difficult the stretch. Next, bend your left leg as if you are trying to sit down and lean forward from the hips, maintaining a neutral spine, until you feel a stretch in your buttock. For a deeper stretch, push down on the inside of your right knee and hold as you bend forward. Switch legs and repeat stretch.

The benefit: The gluteus muscles work hard when you are riding up hills. This stretch maintains their range of motion.

Neck and Back Stretch

The technique: Place both hands shoulder width apart on a picnic table, bench, or hood of a car. Keep your feet shoulder width apart and bend forward from the hips. Remember to keep a neutral spine. Relax your head and neck as you drop your head between your arms. If you are using a bench or fence, grab it with your hands, pull back, and try to lengthen your spine.

The benefit: This stretch feels great, especially if you have been sitting a lot. It reverses the sitting posture and provides a stretch for the back muscles and chest.

Chest Stretch

The technique: Clasp your hands behind your back and pull down.

The benefit: Stretches pectoral muscles, at the front of your chest, and your shoulders.

Active Shoulder Stretch

The technique: Bend your arm ninety degrees, lift your hand to chest level, and point your elbow to the side. Circle your arm over your head and back. Repeat with other arm.

The benefit: Stretches the shoulder muscles and improves or maintains the range of motion in your shoulder joint.

3

Fuelling Up for Biking

Endurance activities like cycling require a constant supply of energy. Your reserves of fat supply some of the calories needed, but you also need some food in your stomach to keep you from fading too quickly. Enjoy a pre-ride snack that combines carbohydrates and protein. Carbohydrates can be simple or complex. Simple carbohydrates, such as a chocolate bar or a slice of white bread, provide lots of sugar but not much nutritional value compared to the number of calories consumed. Complex carbohydrates, like multi-grain bread or dried fruit, provide fibre and vitamins along with the sugars you need for energy. As often as possible, choose complex carbohydrates for optimal energy and nutrition. When choosing protein, look for low-fat options if you are trying to cut back on fat. This chapter provides recipes and nutritional information that will help you choose appropriate snacks for cycling.

ENERGY BARS: THE FACTS

The first energy bar to hit the North American market was the Powerbar® back in the late 1980s. Now grocery stores offer a choice of almost thirty types of energy bars. High-carbohydrate bars claim to provide a steady release of energy, while high-protein bars are supposed to prevent hunger and help the body process sugars. But are these expensive bars any better than a chocolate bar? While chocolate bars inject sugar into the bloodstream, providing a surge of energy quickly followed by a drop in energy, energy bars are supposed to be nutritionally balanced so that blood sugar levels increase and decrease more moderately. Not all bars achieve this goal and many are full of simple sugars, just like a chocolate bar. An energy bar that is not just a chocolate bar in disguise is low in fat (less than five grams of fat per bar) and contains between three and five grams of fibre.

If you choose to consume energy bars as snacks, make sure you also eat some "real food," such as an apple or some milk, since most energy bars are not meal replacements. In the end, it is hard to beat the nutritional benefits of food variety. For example, a sandwich on multi-grain bread full of meats and cheeses or peanut butter and jam provides fat and protein from the meat, cheese, or nuts, carbohydrates from the bread, and if jam is used, some simple sugars that give you a burst of energy. A small container of low-fat yogurt and a piece of fruit provide fat, protein, fibre, and carbohydrates. With a bit of planning, you can avoid high-priced, processed convenience foods. Stay fully fuelled with a tasty and satisfying lunch along the trails.

The Recipes

A little at-home preparation will ensure you are well fuelled before and throughout your ride. The recipes provided below are easy to prepare, store well in the freezer, and are trail-tested. They will make your taste buds sing!

Granola

Start your day with this nutrient-packed homemade cereal and you'll have energy to spare for a long bike ride. Protein and fat from the seeds and nuts, lots of fibre from the oatmeal, and very little sugar make granola the perfect endurance food. It's a staple in my house. This recipe makes four to five litres of granola. Note: You can find unroasted seeds and nuts at either of two Community Natural Foods locations: 1304–10 Avenue SW or at Chinook Station Market, 202–61 Avenue SW.

Preheat oven to 300°F.

Combine the following ingredients in a large heavy roasting pan:

1 cup/250 mL	whole wheat flour
1½ cups/375 mL	skim milk powder
1½ cups/375 mL	unroasted wheat germ
1 cup/250 mL	sesame seeds
6 cups/1.5 L	rolled oats
1 cup/250 mL	shelled unroasted sunflower seeds
1 cup/250 mL	shelled unroasted pumpkin seeds
1 cup/250 mL	Grape Nuts™
1 cup/250 mL	slivered almonds

Combine the following ingredients in a saucepan:

1 cup/250 mL	canola oil
2 tbsp./30 mL	molasses
½ cup/125 mL	honey
1 tsp./5 mL	vanilla

Warm over low heat to blend. Drizzle onto granola mixture (a little at a time), stirring as you drizzle. Roast the mixture for 45 to 60 minutes, stirring every 15 minutes at first, then more frequently, until it is golden (not dark) brown. Remove from the oven and cool.

After the granola has cooled, add:

2 cups/500 mL	currants
1 cup/250 mL	chopped dried apricots
1 cup/250 mL	coconut

Store granola in a tightly covered container in cool, dry place.

Pumpkin Molasses Chocolate Loaf

This firm loaf freezes well, so make a double batch. It's packed with goodness and has just enough chocolate in it to entice the kids. Grab a slice as you head out the door for your next urban cycling adventure.

Preheat oven to 350°F.

Spray a 9 x 5 inch (2 L) loaf pan with vegetable oil.

1¼ cup/310 mL	brown sugar
⅓ cup/80 mL	butter
2	eggs
2 tbsp./30 mL	molasses
1 tsp./5 mL	vanilla
1 cup/250 mL	canned pumpkin purée
½ cup/125 mL	raisins
½ cup/125 mL	chocolate.chips
1⅓ cups/330 mL	all-purpose flour
⅔ cup/160 mL	whole wheat flour
2¼ tsp./12 mL	cinnamon
1½ tsp./7 mL	baking powder
½ tsp./2 mL	baking soda
¼ tsp./1 mL	ginger
½ cup/125 mL	1% or 2% yogurt

1. In a large bowl, beat sugar and butter together until crumbly. Add eggs and mix until smooth. Beat in molasses, vanilla, and pumpkin (mixture may appear curdled). Stir in raisins and chocolate chips.

2. In another bowl, combine flour, cinnamon, baking powder, baking soda, and ginger.

3. Add dry ingredients to wet ingredients alternately with the yogurt; stir just until combined. Pour into pan and bake for 60 to 70 minutes or until cake tester comes out clean.

Banana Date Muffins

Dates and bananas are the perfect energy foods for a long bike ride. These muffins are rich and moist, and they are a great way to use up those ripe bananas in the freezer.

Preheat oven to 375°F.

Spray twelve muffin cups with vegetable oil.

¼ cup/60 mL	butter
1	medium banana, mashed
¾ cup/185 mL	granulated sugar
1	egg
1 tsp./5 mL	vanilla
¾ cup/185 mL	whole wheat flour
½ cup/125 mL	bran flakes, corn flakes, or granola (for that extra crunch!)
1 tsp./5 mL	baking powder
1 tsp./5 mL	baking soda
¾ cup/185 mL	chopped pitted dates
½ cup/125 mL	plain yogurt (non-fat or 2%)

1. In a large bowl, combine butter, banana, sugar, egg, and vanilla; mix well.

2. In another bowl, combine flour, cereal, baking powder, and baking soda.

3. Add dry ingredients to wet ingredients and stir until mixed. Stir in dates and yogurt, just until smooth.

4. Spoon batter into prepared muffin cups and bake for 15 to 17 minutes, or until tops are firm and a tester inserted in the centre of a muffin comes out clean.

NOTES:

· Muffins will be fairly flat because of the dates.

· Dates can be replaced with dried apricots, prunes, or raisins.

· Prepare up to one day ahead or freeze for up to three weeks.

Chocolate Chip Oatmeal Cookies

This chocolatey treat is a one-bowl wonder guaranteed to bring smiles to the faces of the kids and adults on your cycling outing. My husband thinks these are the best chocolate chip cookies on the planet. They freeze well, so double the recipe if you have many mouths to feed.

Preheat oven to 325°F.

TIP: Buy top-quality semi-sweet chocolate chips like Safeway Select, President's Choice, or Bernard Callebaut for truly decadent cookies.

1 cup/250 mL	butter
1 cup/250 mL	brown sugar
1 cup/250 mL	white sugar
2	eggs
½ tsp./2 mL	salt
1 tsp./5 mL	baking powder
1 tsp./5 mL	baking soda
1 tsp./5 mL	vanilla
1 cup/250 mL	whole wheat flour
1 cup/250 mL	white flour
2½ cups/625 mL	oatmeal
1½ - 12 oz./300 g	packages chocolate chips

1. In a large bowl, cream butter, brown sugar, and white sugar. Add the eggs and blend. Stir in salt, baking powder, baking soda, vanilla, and flour.
2. Add oatmeal and chocolate chips.
3. Place golf ball-sized cookies on an ungreased baking sheet. Bake for 12 to 15 minutes.

Makes 3 dozen cookies.

4

The Biking Routes

Urban biking is a wonderful activity for families, friends, or individual cyclists. When riding on Calgary's pathways and roads, you are never far from civilization, but at times you feel as if you are in the heart of the wilderness. The routes in this book vary in distance and extend to all corners of Calgary. What is enjoyable for some will not be for others, so I have tried to provide a great variety of routes.

Hidden Gems off the Paved Path: The paved regional pathway system in Calgary is extensive, picturesque, and a joy to use. For many of the routes described, it is the freeway that leads to the hidden gems. Just off the well-used paved paths are pleasant side streets, interesting architecture, mini-parks, funky shopping districts, ethnic eateries, and independently owned cafés and delis serving tasty homemade food and great coffee.

Neighbourhood Routes with Character: Many routes in this book combine paved pathway riding with visits to Calgary's more established neighbourhoods. Quiet, tree-lined streets, colourful gardens, and interesting architecture are reasons to slow down to a leisurely pace. Historic communities with pop-bottle stucco wartime homes, large vegetable gardens, and streets that dip and climb to wonderful viewpoints make these routes pleasant pedalling.

After-Work, Half-Day, and Full-Day Rides: The great thing about biking in Calgary is that it's close to home. Choose your ride based on the time you have available. Post-work rides can be as short as half an hour to explore a natural area such as Griffith Woods, or two hours long to travel from Wildwood to Bridgeland. Half-day outings can be long routes where you pedal steadily, or shorter routes that leave time to stop for lunch, a coffee, or a break at the playground. Full-day outings let you explore the north, south, or all of Calgary in one day.

Categories

Each bike route in this book has been classified into one or more of the following categories.

CATEGORY	EXPLANATION
Family	Routes follow the paved or gravel pathways or quiet streets.
Kids	Kids enjoy these routes, which follow paved or gravel pathways and may have playground stops or interesting play areas.
Bike trailer–friendly	Routes follow paved or gravel path paths or quiet streets, and always have a crosswalk option at busy street intersections. These routes were tested using a Chariot Carrier bike trailer for two children.
Paved pathway	Routes follow the paved pathways.
Neighbourhood	Routes follow quiet streets through neighbourhoods.
Nature	Routes offer solitude in nature. Wildlife, birds, creeks, and wildflowers are a big part of these outings.
Culture	These urban routes offer side trips to interesting shopping, eating, and people-watching districts.
Rollerblade	All or portions of these routes are perfect for rollerblading.
Non-stop	These routes follow the paved regional pathway system for the most part and have no or very few stops at intersections.
Hill training	Hill climbs on these routes allow for physical conditioning.
Ice cream	An ice cream stop is located along or near these routes.
Lunch	Lunch locations that offer packable picnic food or tasty and quick eat-in fare are available along these routes.
Picnic	Picnic tables are available for a lunch stop along these routes.
Coffee shop	A cozy café is recommended on these routes for that pre-, post-, or middle-of-the-ride pit stop.

Degree of Difficulty

Pacing is the key to an enjoyable bike ride. You can slow down and enjoy a leisurely ride past homes and gardens or work up a sweat on a quiet, paved pathway with few stops. Be sure to review Chapter Two prior to exploring any route described in this book if you have been inactive for awhile. You should never feel nauseated or light-headed when exercising. Listen to your body and have a safe and enjoyable urban bike ride.

FITNESS LEVEL OF ROUTE	EXPLANATION	CHOOSING A ROUTE FOR YOUR FITNESS LEVEL (see page 17 for zone details)
Easy	Mostly flat; under 10 kilometres	If you are just starting an exercise program, choose a bike trail at this level and keep your heart rate in Zone 1. You should always be able to carry on a conversation while exercising in this zone.
Moderate	A combination of flats and hills, or a very long, flat ride.	These routes will demand more cardiovascular conditioning either because of the one or more hill climbs throughout the route or because of the distance covered. It should be easy to maintain your heart rate in Zones 1 or 2 during the ride. When climbing hills, your heart rate may be in Zones 3 or 4.
Challenging	Lots of hills throughout and/or very long routes.	These rides require a high level of cardiovascular and muscular fitness. Do not attempt these routes on your first outing of the season.

Trail Etiquette and Safety

Prevent Trail Erosion

I recommend established pathways in all of the routes described in this book. But pathways can change, based on new management plans developed each year by the City of Calgary parks department. The parks department develops new trails and reclaims old ones to prevent erosion. In order to keep our parks intact for future generations, please avoid paths that are closed even if they are included in the routes in this book.

Flowers and Wildlife

Stop and smell the flowers, but don't pick them! Leave them for others to enjoy. Never, ever feed wildlife. Coyotes, deer, and bears are wild animals and can be dangerous. If you feed them, they may start to demand food from other people, which increases the potential for unhappy encounters between people and wildlife. When wildlife demand food, they are considered aggressive, dangerous, and a threat to people, and are usually terminated. So don't feed the animals and let them live a long and happy life!

Paved Pathway Safety

As when you drive, stay on the right-hand side of the path. Ring your bell and announce, "on your left" when passing anyone, even when there is lots of space for you to pass. The warning of your approach ensures you won't startle someone.

Biking Alone

Seeking peace and solitude is one reason to hit the urban trails. Be aware, however, that when you are far from the hustle and bustle, you are also far from help if you need it. Bring a friend or let someone know your planned route before you head out alone.

Biking in Winter

The routes in this book are intended for leisure. I know that some people cycle year-round in Calgary, but many of the routes described combine neighbourhood streets with paved paths. Since side streets are not cleared of snow at any time of year, and only some of the paved pathways are cleared of snow, I do not recommend biking any of these routes in the winter. I advise you to use caution in the spring, when parts of the bike pathways are still covered in snow.

Cycling and Rollerblade Safety

It is absolutely critical that all cyclists and rollerbladers wear a helmet. There have been many rollerblade head injuries and subsequent deaths on Calgary pathways in the past few years. If you are not extremely proficient on rollerblades, do not attempt hills or even slight declines. Your head will take the brunt of the fall when you lose your balance. If you are not wearing a helmet, a simple fall could mean a brain injury or death. Rollerbladers should also consider wearing elbow and knee pads to help cushion a fall.

Legend

ROUTE PATHWAY

| paved road | paved path | unpaved path |

NEARBY PATHWAYS

| paved road | paved path | unpaved path |

route continuance between map plates

parking	P	tree	
restroom	R	fence	x x x
bike start	X	power line	
footbridge	■	picnic area	
traffic bridge	□	playgound	
sign	⇨	on-leash area	
viewpoint		off-leash area	
LRT station		coffee shop	
LRT	—–—–	landmark building	
railroad		school	
tunnel	●	downslope	
traffic light	⁝	ice cream	
flashing light		food	

Calgary's Best Short Bike Rides

(approximate route start location and loop length)

ROUTES

1 Baker Park/Bowness (6 km)
2 Edgemont Park Ravines (6 km)
3 Airport (12 km)
4 Confederation Park (4 km)
5 Elliston Regional Park (3 km)
6 Griffith Woods (6 km)

BAKER PARK/ BOWNESS PARK, NW

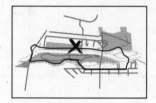

Categories: *paved pathway, nature, family, bike trailer–friendly, kids, rollerblade, non-stop, picnic, ice cream*
Approximate Distance: *6 kilometres*
Terrain: *paved path, quiet street*
Degree of Difficulty: *easy*
Parking: *Baker Park official parking lot at 9333 Scenic Bow Road NW*
Facilities: *bathrooms, playgrounds, water parks, picnic tables, firepits*
Ice Cream: *Angel's Drive Inn, corner of 47 Avenue and 85 Street NW*

Route at a Glance

Travel the smooth Bow River Pathway from Baker Park to just short of Bowmont Natural Environment Park. A couple of pedestrian bridges nestled amongst the poplars lead to the south side of the river. The quiet streets of Bowness make for a relaxing ride that leads kids to their first goal, the ice cream stop! Angel's Drive Inn, at the halfway point of the route, makes for a nice snack or supper stop. Grab your goodies to go and enjoy a picnic lunch in Bowness Park. This multi-use park has a tiny train for the kids to ride, canoe rentals on the lagoon, a few playgrounds, and a water park. Follow the shale path along the lagoon through the trees to the paved pathway. The impressive Stoney Trail bridge towers above the pedestrian bridge that takes you back to the north side of the river, where a short, rolling ride on smooth trails leads back to the car.

Cautions/Highlights

The route is long enough to challenge young children a bit but short enough that they will be back to the car before exhaustion sets in. Bowness Park is very popular in the summer so prepare for crowded trails.

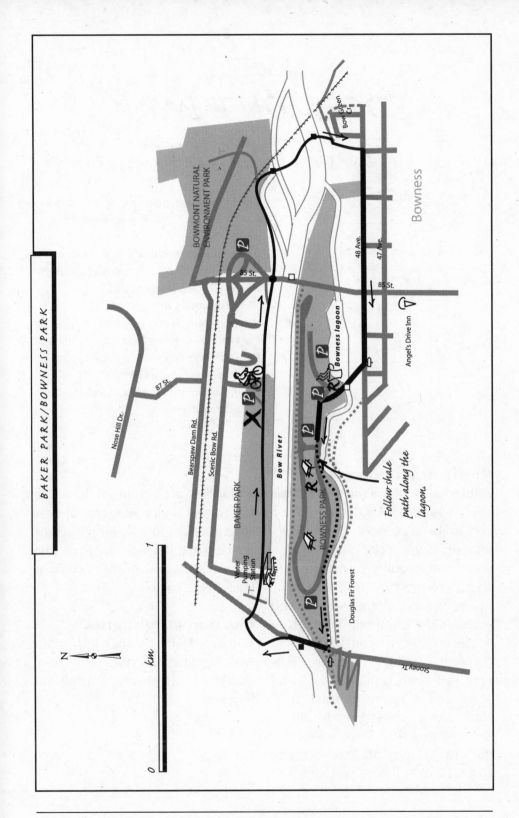

EDGEMONT PARK RAVINES, NW

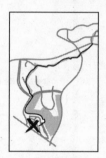

Categories: *paved pathway, nature, family, bike trailer–friendly, kids, rollerblade, picnic, ice cream*

Approximate Distance: *no set route; end to end, the park is approximately 3 kilometres long, or 6 kilometres round trip*

Terrain: *paved path*

Degree of Difficulty: *easy*

Parking: *park in the official parking lot on the west side of Edgemont Drive, just north of John Laurie Boulevard NW*

Facilities: *bathrooms, playgrounds, picnic tables, firepits*

Route at a Glance

Hidden in the ravine below the hilltop homes of Edgemont is a picture-perfect park that boasts lots of scenic variety. The route starts out heading north through the manicured ravine park. Enjoy green grass, playgrounds, and a gradually climbing path. At a T intersection, continue west through a wildlife corridor. This area has been kept in its natural state and is home to mule deer that feed amongst the shrubbery and coyotes that often cross the pathways. Listen for bird calls rising from the cattail-lined wetland that is the next attraction on the route. If a tunnel under Shaganappi Trail sounds like fun, then continue north. Turn back at any time and enjoy a rolling pathway all the way back to the car.

Cautions/Highlights

The paved path through Edgemont Park Ravines is not very busy, making it a relaxing outing for families.

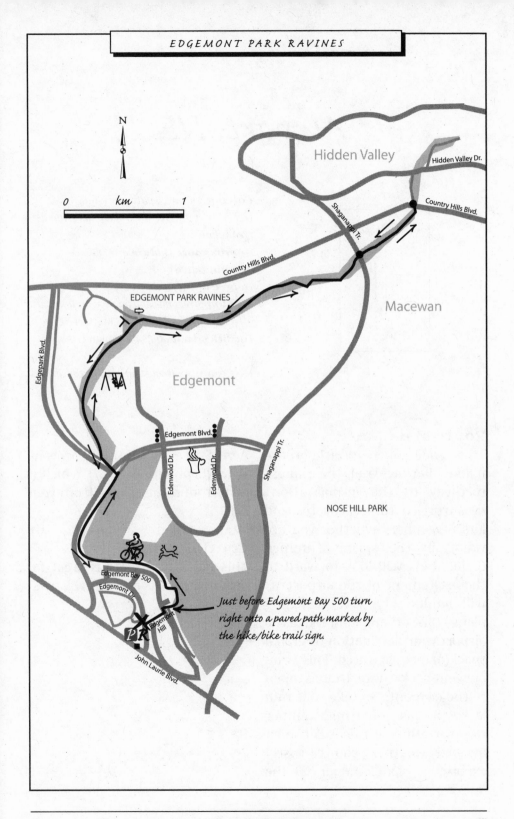

N

0   km   1

Hidden Valley

Hidden Valley Dr.

Country Hills Blvd.

Shaganappi Tr.

Country Hills Blvd.

EDGEMONT PARK RAVINES

Macewan

Edgepark Blvd.

Edgemont

Edgemont Blvd.

Edenwold Dr.

Edenwold Dr.

Shaganappi Tr.

NOSE HILL PARK

Edgemont Bay 500

Edgemont Dr.

Edgemont Hill

P R

John Laurie Blvd.

Just before Edgemont Bay 500 turn right onto a paved path marked by the hike/bike trail sign.

Airport, NE

Categories: *paved pathway, family, bike trailer–friendly, kids, rollerblade, non-stop, ice cream, lunch*
Approximate Distance: *12 kilometres*
Terrain: *paved path*
Degree of Difficulty: *easy*
Parking: *street parking on Pegasus Road, just off McKnight Boulevard and 19 Street NE*
Facilities: *bathrooms, playgrounds (both at airport)*
Ice Cream: *food court upstairs at the airport*

Route at a Glance

This wide open prairie route follows Barlow Trail, the express roadway to the airport. Don't be surprised to see coyotes and lots of gophers whether you are riding in the spring, summer, or fall. Kids will look forward to the excitement of the airport, as will adults who love watching planes take off and land. Make the airport your destination to grab a snack or people-watch. This is an out-and-back route that is open to the elements, so take your rain jacket in case of a mid-summer rainstorm. If your ride is cut short by bad weather, you can still experience planes indoors at the Aero Space Museum (4629 McCall Way NE; phone: 250-3752), which is just around the corner from your car.

Cautions/Highlights

This flat, paved route is great for beginner cyclists and rollerbladers.

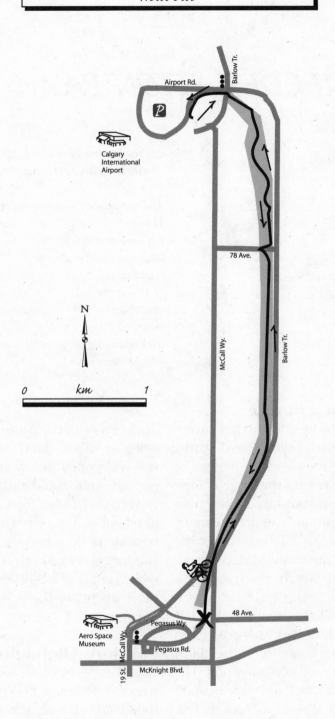

CONFEDERATION PARK, NW

Categories: *paved pathway, nature, family, bike trailer–friendly, kids, rollerblade, picnic, ice cream*

Approximate Distance: *no set route; up to 4 kilometres*

Terrain: *paved path*

Degree of Difficulty: *easy*

Parking: *official parking lots at 10 Street and 24 Avenue NW*

Facilities: *bathrooms, playgrounds, picnic tables*

Ice Cream: *Shivers Hard Ice Cream (1840–20 Avenue NW)*

Route at a Glance

A park with lots of water is always popular with kids. Paved paths make for easy cycling along the creek that travels the length of the park. Get off your bike to play with the kids around or under the many small bridges that criss-cross the creek. You can throw sticks or make boats and watch them float to Nose Creek in the northeast, which is where all that water is headed. Confederation Park was created in 1967 to commemorate the 100th anniversary of Confederation. The constructed wetland just west of 10 Street NW, with its cattails, red-winged blackbirds, and families of ducks, is one of the park's highlights. Bring a picnic lunch and enjoy the wide open grassy hillsides, or perhaps you would rather choose to spread out your feast in a shady oasis under a poplar tree. This is a popular park, especially on warm summer evenings and on weekends, when people of all shapes and sizes move about on the pathways and green spaces.

Cautions/Highlights

This a safe place to take people who are learning how to ride or rollerblade. It's also a wonderful park for picnics.

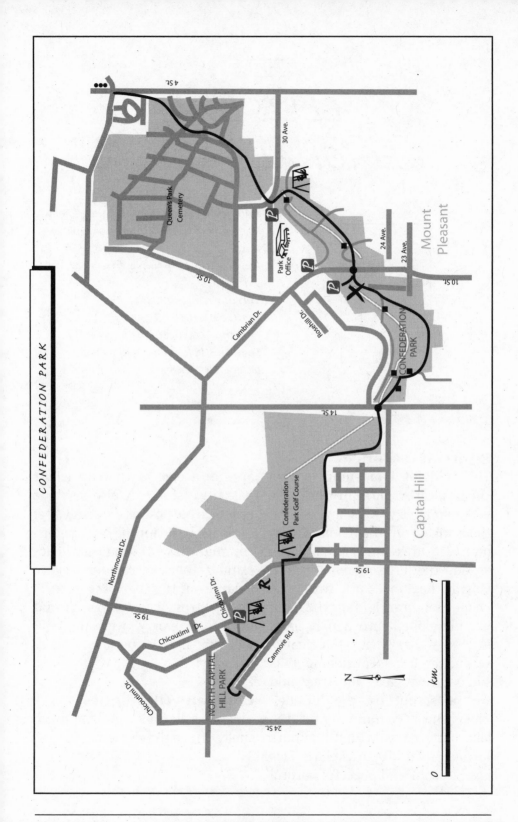

ELLISTON REGIONAL PARK, SE

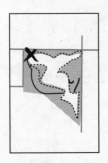

Categories: *paved pathway, nature, family, bike trailer–friendly, kids, rollerblade, picnic, ice cream*
Approximate Distance: *no set route; 1 to 3 kilometres*
Terrain: *paved path, dirt path*
Degree of Difficulty: *easy*
Parking: *17 Avenue and 60 Street SE*
Facilities: *bathrooms, playgrounds, picnic tables, firepits*

Route at a Glance

There's a lot happening in this small prairie park in the east end of Calgary. Kids love riding their bikes on the combination of paved, dirt, and grass paths around the large man-made lake. Elliston Regional Park was once wide open prairie, but the land was developed into a hilly oasis in 1994 and now boasts Calgary's second-largest lake. Rolling hills surround the lake, and trees and shrubs sprout on the hillsides. The pathway circumnavigates the lake, with many dirt-path detours for kids who like to explore. This is a pleasant and peaceful natural area in a part of the city where parks are scarce. It also serves a practical purpose as a storm-water drainage basin for the surrounding communities. During a heavy rainfall, the lake can increase in volume at the alarming rate of 35,000 litres of water per second. But don't worry, warning bells will ring before the lake reaches capacity!

Cautions/Highlights

This park does not provide much shelter from the elements.

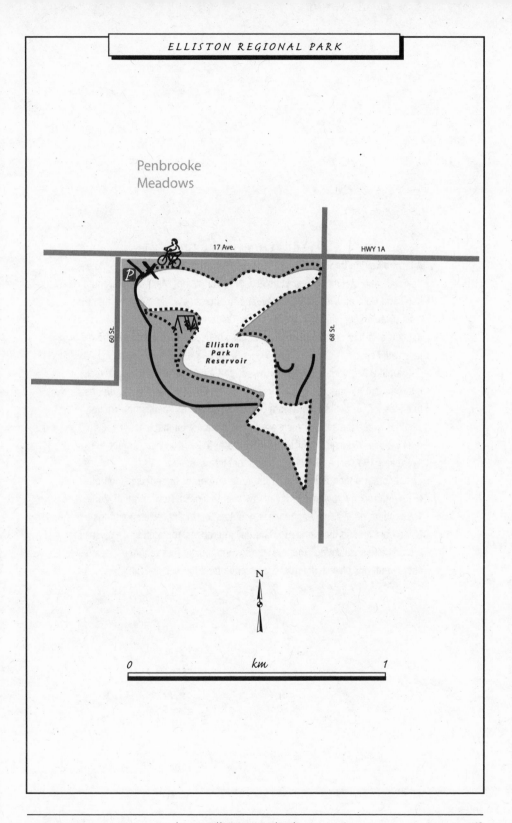

Penbrooke
Meadows

17 Ave.

HWY 1A

60 St.

69 St.

Elliston
Park
Reservoir

N

0   km   1

INTERNATIONAL AVENUE

After a bike ride through Elliston Regional Park, you can take a trip to India, Pakistan, the Mediterranean, Jamaica, Newfoundland, Mexico, Nicaragua, Italy, and Germany. International Avenue in Forest Lawn is the most ethnically diverse shopping and eating area in Calgary, partly because it is home to such a variety of cultural groups and also because the area offers affordable retail space.

Unlike Kensington in the northwest and 17 Avenue in the southwest, International Avenue, with its four lanes of traffic and many busy turnoffs to shops, is not pedestrian-friendly. The cost to make it pedestrian-friendly would drive up the cost for retail space and drive out all that is unique about International Avenue. When travelling here by bike, it is best to follow 19 Avenue or 16 Avenue SE to find a shop that interests you.

Another option is to explore the area on one of the popular food bus tours offered by the International Avenue Business Revitalization Zone. These tours offer a fun way to learn how to shop for ingredients and taste foods from around the world. On Saturday afternoons, fourteen times a year, the bus takes salivating "tourists" on a world tour to five continents spanning twenty-six blocks. (International Avenue food tours: 248-7288)

SHOPPING AND LUNCH TIPS

Hungry after your visit to Elliston Regional Park? Zip down to AAA Jamaica Cuisine & Donair (20, 5315–17 Avenue SE) for a top-notch donair. Some of my favourite shopping stops are close by. For example, Calgary Spiceland (130, 1830–52 Street SE) sells spices at incredible value and offers everything you need to cook Indian cuisine. For an immediate taste of Indian food, try the Skylark restaurant (5315–17 Avenue SE), just around the corner from Spiceland. Their vegetarian samosas are very tasty and are great in a picnic lunch. For those of you with a sweet tooth, make sure to stop at Gunther's Fine Baking (4306–17 Avenue SE). This unassuming concrete building is the home of high-quality German baked goods. Tarts, marzipan-wrapped cream cakes dusted in cocoa, and cream-filled mouse-shaped treats are all prepared daily. So plan your attack and visit a shop or two after your ride. It's a cultural adventure in the heart of the city.

GRIFFITH WOODS, SW

Categories: *paved pathway, nature, family, bike trailer–friendly, kids, picnic, rollerblade*
Approximate Distance: *6 kilometres*
Terrain: *paved path, dirt path*
Degree of Difficulty: *easy*
Parking: *From Highway 8, turn south onto Discovery Ridge Boulevard, then south onto Discovery Ridge Link; official parking lot at the south end of Discovery Ridge Link SW*
Rollerblade Route: *The flat, wide, smooth paved path is perfect for beginners who need to master their skills. Travel up and back on the paved path.*
Facilities: *bathrooms*

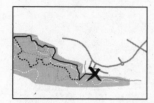

Route at a Glance

If you need a dose of pure nature, head to Griffith Woods for a bike ride or a stroll. This 92-hectare natural area is hidden below Glenmore Trail in a new housing development called Discovery Ridge. The parkland in Griffith Woods, donated to the city by the Griffith family in 2000, represents the largest private land donation in Calgary's history. Even though Wilbur Griffith was an avid golfer, he decided that this piece of nature surrounding the Elbow River should be kept in its natural state for all to enjoy. Griffith Woods is one of three "special protection" natural areas in the city. The other two are the Inglewood Bird Sanctuary and Weaselhead Flats.

The cycling route here follows a combination of paved and gravel pathways that weave back and forth over the Elbow River. Beaver dams create ponds along the route, and if you sit quietly at dawn or dusk you may see the beavers at work. Kids love the chance to get off their bikes and throw stones or sticks into the many creeks and ponds. Large evergreens and poplar trees provide shade throughout the ride. Griffith Woods is the only place in Calgary that floods almost every year, and since poplars need yearly flooding to thrive, they do

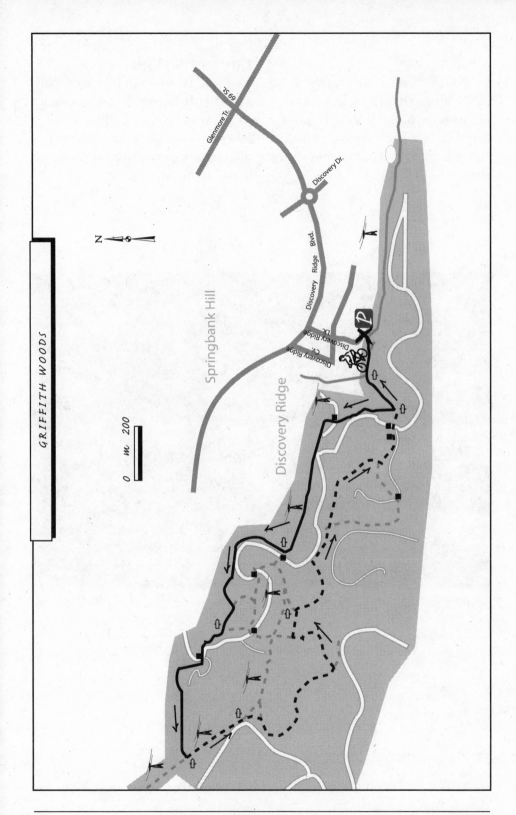

Springbank Hill

Discovery Ridge

Glenmore Tr.

Sarcee Tr.

Discovery Dr.

Discovery Ridge Blvd.

Discovery Ridge Cir.

Discovery Ridge Lk.

N

0   m   200

very well here. Interpretive signs describing the flora, fauna, and ecosystems along part of the route are just one more reason to slow the pace, look around, and enjoy nature in the city.

Cautions/Highlights

The flat, wide, smooth paved path at Griffith Woods is a great place to go with young children riding bikes, rollerblading, or riding in a bike trailer. Dogs must be kept on a leash in the park.

A pond in Griffith Woods is perfectly still on a lazy summer day.

Calgary's Best Medium-length Bike Rides

(approximate route start location and loop length)

Stoney Trail · Country · Hills · Boulevard · WEST NOSE CREEK PARK · 8 · Airport · Barlow Trail · Edgemont Boulevard · Beddington Trail · Crowchild · Sarcee Trail · John · Laurie · 10 · 9 · NOSE HILL PARK · 64 Avenue · 14 Street · Boulevard · McKnight Boulevard · BOWMONT PARK · BOWNESS PARK · 7 11 · University of Calgary · CONFEDERATION PARK · 12 · Centre Street · Edmonton Trail · Deerfoot · N · CANADA OLYMPIC PARK · 14 · 15 · Trans-Canada · Highway · 16 · Memorial · 13 · zoo · Drive · 17 Avenue · EDWORTHY PARK · Bow · River · Downtown · 17 · 18 · ELLISTON REGIONAL PARK · 60 Street · 68 Street · 0 km 5 · Saddledome · Elbow River · INGLEWOOD BIRD SANCTUARY · Trail · Sarcee Trail · 33 Avenue · 19 · 20 · Irrigation · Discovery Ridge · RIVER PARK · GRIFFITH WOODS · 6 · Boulevard · Glenmore · Trail · Macleod Trail · Elbow Drive · CARBURN PARK · 23 · Canal

ROUTES BY NUMBER

7 Bowmont Park/Scenic Acres Ravines (17 km)
8 West Nose Creek Park/Nose Hill Park (21 km)
9 Nose Hill Park (Flat) (12 km)
10 Nose Hill Park (Hilly) (13 km)
11 Bowness/Bowmont Park (15 km)
12 Confederation Park/Nose Hill Park (23 km)
13 Nose Creek/West Nose Creek Park (22 km)
14 Patterson Heights/Strathcona/ Edworthy Park (15 km)
15 Wildwood/Bridgeland (30 km)
16 Sunnyside/Confederation Park/ Parksdale (20 km)
17 Inglewood/Mount Royal/ Scotsman's Hill (20 km)
18 Inglewood Bird Sanctuary/ Carburn Park (17 km)
19 Garrison Woods/Mount Royal/ Glenmore Reservoir (30 km)
20 Mount Royal/River Valley/Knob Hill (19 km)
21 Glenmore Reservoir/Fish Creek Provincial Park (20 km)

22 Glenmore Reservoir (16.5 km)
23 Carburn Park/Douglasdale/ Fish Creek Provincial Park (17 km)
24 Fish Creek Provincial Provincial Park, West End (16 km)
25 Fish Creek Provincial Park/McKenzie/ Douglasdale (23 km)
26 Fish Creek Park, East End (19 km)

Glenmore Reservoir · 22 · 21 · 24 Street · 14 Street · Elbow Drive · Anderson Road · 37 Street · Canyon · Meadows · Bow Bottom Trail · Drive · 26 · FISH CREEK PROVINCIAL PARK · 25 · 22 X · Deerfoot Trail

ROUTE 7

BOWMONT NATURAL ENVIRONMENT PARK/ SCENIC ACRES RAVINES, NW

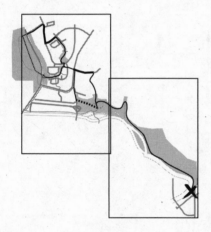

Categories: *neighbourhood, paved pathway, nature, family, kids, picnic*
Approximate Distance: *17 kilometres*
Terrain: *quiet street, paved path, dirt path*
Degree of Difficulty: *moderate with hill climbs throughout*
Parking: *Bowmont Natural Environment Park (east end); park in the official parking area just off Home Road on 52 Street NW*
Facilities: *playgrounds*

Route at a Glance

Start with a smooth ride along the Bow River Pathway through Bowmont Natural Environment Park. Look across the river to the large lots with million-dollar homes in the community of Bowness, which is blessed with this piece of natural heaven in the heart of the city. A gradual hill climb leads to the first view of the Rockies. Enjoy a brief downhill glide before turning and climbing up a narrow treed valley that leads into Silver Springs.

The shade in the valley is a welcome relief on a hot summer day. Wildflower-covered hillsides are in full bloom during July and August, and in June the abundance of flowering wolf willow imparts a pungent aroma. A short stint on quiet streets leads to more paved paths in Scenic Acres. These community pathways lead you through ravines along the backyards of a neighbourhood full of impressive vegetable and flower gardens. Pass by playing fields and into a lush wild-ravine wetland that is alive with birds and cattails and hillsides dotted with purple flax, pink wild roses, and yellow potentilla. Continue on the streets of Scenic Acres until you reach the energy-efficient house that stands out from the rest. No city water, sewer, or gas hookups for these homeowners; they use solar energy to heat and power their home, a composting toilet, and water barrels to collect the rain. Impressive!

Now pedal downhill on paved paths to the green space parallel to Stoney Trail. Ride the dirt trail along the wide ridge and enjoy the mountain views before you drop down and under Stoney Trail into another full-leaf ravine. A short stint on a narrow path leads to the paved paths, and soon you are winding along a creek and appreciating the beautiful backyards of the lucky homeowners in Scenic Acres. A quick downhill ride along the pathway parallel to Nose Hill Drive leads back into Bowmont park, where a dirt road leads to the paved Bow River Pathway. One last hill climb gets the heart rate up and makes coasting back to the car even more enjoyable. The last part of the trail along the river's edge offers you the opportunity to get off your bike and cool your toes in the glacial waters of the Bow River.

Cautions/Highlights

Some of this route is comprised of bumpy dirt trails. You will need a mountain bike to travel the entire route.

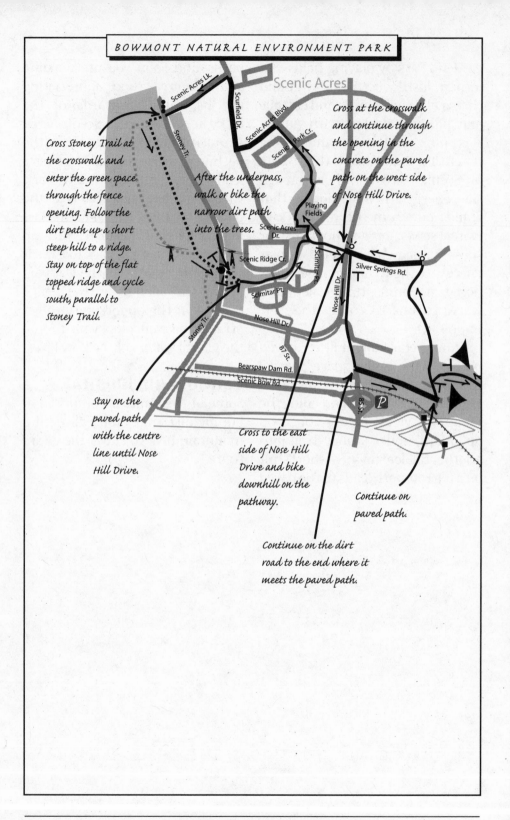

Scenic Acres

Cross Stoney Trail at the crosswalk and enter the green space through the fence opening. Follow the dirt path up a short steep hill to a ridge. Stay on top of the flat topped ridge and cycle south, parallel to Stoney Trail.

After the underpass, walk or bike the narrow dirt path into the trees.

Cross at the crosswalk and continue through the opening in the concrete on the paved path on the west side of Nose Hill Drive.

Scenic Acres Lk.

Stoney Tr.

Scurfield Dr.

Scenic Acres Blvd.

Scenic Park Cr.

Playing Fields

Scenic Acres Dr.

Scimitar Pt.

Scenic Ridge Cr.

Scimitar Pt.

Nose Hill Dr.

Silver Springs Rd.

Nose Hill Dr.

Stoney Tr.

87 St.

Bearspaw Dam Rd.

Scenic Bow Rd

85 St.

Stay on the paved path with the centre line until Nose Hill Drive.

Cross to the east side of Nose Hill Drive and bike downhill on the pathway.

Continue on paved path.

Continue on the dirt road to the end where it meets the paved path.

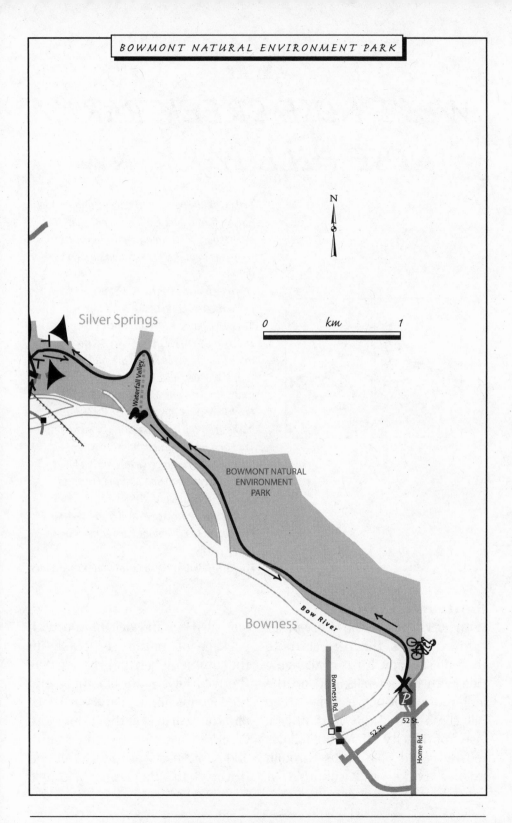

WEST NOSE CREEK PARK/ NOSE HILL PARK, NW

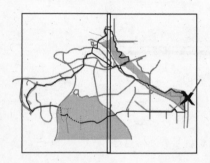

Categories: *paved pathway, neighbourhood, nature, family, bike trailer–friendly, kids, rollerblade, hill training, picnic, lunch, coffee shop (see Route 12, "Friends Cappuccino Bar" for details)*

Approximate Distance: *Short Route: 19 kilometres; Long Route: 21 kilometres*

Terrain: *paved path, dirt path*

Degree of Difficulty: *Short Route: moderate/difficult, lots of gradual hills and a couple of steep hills; Long Route: same as short route but with one more steep hill*

Parking: *West Nose Creek Park, official parking lot at the intersection of Beddington Trail and Beddington Boulevard NE; or Nose Hill Edgemont, official parking lot at the intersection of Shaganappi Trail and Edgemont Boulevard NW*

Rollerblade Route: *travel from West Nose Creek Park to Edgemont Park Ravines on paved paths*

Facilities: *bathrooms, playgrounds, picnic tables*

Route at a Glance

With very few stops or other cyclists, this is the perfect route to pedal quickly. It's a challenging ride with lots of hills, and on the long-route option, a very steep hill climb that leads to fantastic views of the city. This route follows mostly paved bike paths through ravines, parks, and suburbia. It will surprise and delight you with pockets of nature, especially in the summer, when the grass is green, the wildflowers are blooming, and the lagoons are lush and alive with birds and cattails. In the spring, Nose Creek is fast moving and murky, and some parts are more full and frothy than others since a couple of beaver families reside along the water. Those beavers have to rely on shrubs for building materials since trees are scarce along this route.

West Nose Creek Park is the takeoff point. Travel through the neighbourhoods west of the park and imagine what they would look like with big trees. At the same time, remember that this area is typical of the Prairies, and the absence of large evergreens and leafy trees is just a part of the landscape. Summer is the most colourful time along Nose Creek. You may wish to bike this route in April if you have a passion for shades of brown!

If you choose the long-route option with the extra large hill, you will be rewarded with a great view. Once you've tackled that hill, head up to the top of the sandstone outcrops to the north to enjoy views of the city. Both short and long routes lead to Edgemont Park Ravines, a wildlife corridor that has been kept in its natural state. Tunnels under major roads allow cyclists and animals to travel freely in this area. Nonchalant coyotes may cross the path without warning (I almost hit one once!), and mule deer eat and rest in the shrubbery throughout the ravine. A manicured ravine park with playgrounds, landscaped ponds, and picnic tables follows on the heels of the wilderness ravine.

Climb to Nose Hill Park, Calgary's highest point and the largest urban natural environment park in Canada. Mountain views are stunning in the spring, when snow highlights the majestic peaks. The nice thing about climbing to the highest point in Calgary is the gradual descent that follows. Soak up nature while coasting down through the park and beyond. Follow the bike path through neighbourhoods back to West Nose Creek Park.

An interesting art installation in Edgemont Park Ravines combines urban artistry and nature.

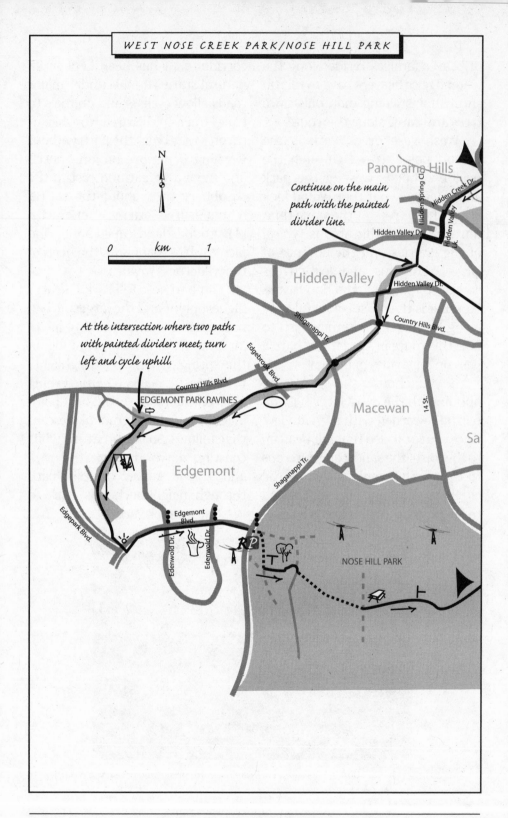

Continue on the main
path with the painted
divider line.

At the intersection where two paths
with painted dividers meet, turn
left and cycle uphill.

Panorama Hills

Hidden Creek Dr.

Hidden Spring Cir.

Hidden Valley Lk.

Hidden Valley Dr.

Hidden Valley

Hidden Valley Dr.

Shaganappi Tr.

Country Hills Blvd.

Edgebrook Blvd.

Country Hills Blvd.

EDGEMONT PARK RAVINES

Macewan

14 St.

Sa

Edgemont

Shaganappi Tr.

Edgemont Blvd.

Edenwold Dr.

Edenwold Dr.

Edgepark Blvd.

NOSE HILL PARK

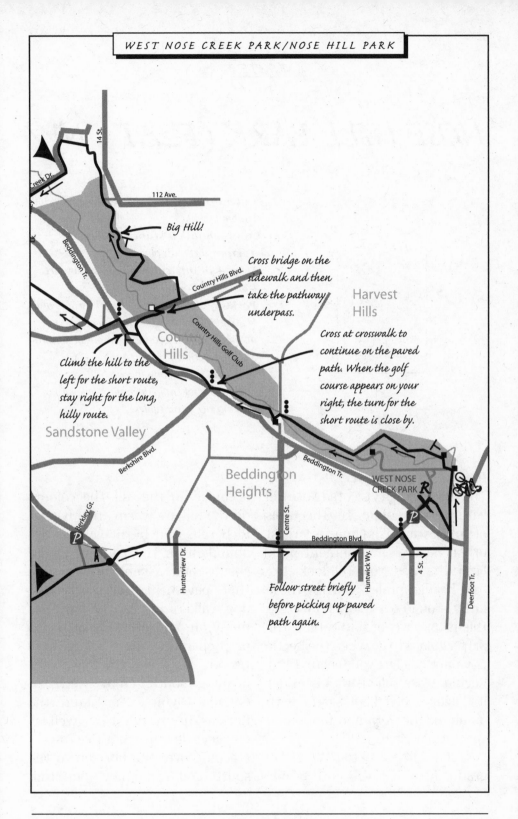

112 Ave.

14 St.

Creek Dr.

Beddington Tr.

Big Hill!

Country Hills Blvd.

Cross bridge on the sidewalk and then take the pathway underpass.

Harvest Hills

Country Hills Golf Club

Country Hills

Cross at crosswalk to continue on the paved path. When the golf course appears on your right, the turn for the short route is close by.

Climb the hill to the left for the short route, stay right for the long, hilly route.

Sandstone Valley

Berkshire Blvd.

Beddington Tr.

WEST NOSE CREEK PARK

Beddington Heights

Berkley Gt.

P

Centre St.

P

Beddington Blvd.

Hunterview Dr.

Huntwick Wy.

4 St.

Deerfoot Tr.

Follow street briefly before picking up paved path again.

NOSE HILL PARK (FLAT), NW

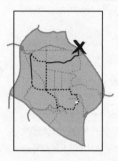

Categories: *nature, family, kids, non-stop, hill training, picnic*
Approximate Distance: *12 kilometres*
Terrain: *dirt path, paved path*
Degree of Difficulty: *easy on bumpy dirt trails*
Parking: *official parking at Berkley Gate and 14 Street NW intersection; or, official parking at Shaganappi Trail and Edgemont Boulevard NW intersection*
Facilities: *bathrooms (on west side of park at Shaganappi Trail/Edgemont Boulevard parking lot), picnic tables*

Route at a Glance

The City of Calgary created Nose Hill Park in 1973. Spanning 1,093 hectares of prairiescape, it is Canada's largest urban natural environment park. From the road, Nose Hill looks like bald-headed prairie, but for those lucky enough to explore it up close, this is an oasis of natural life, the perfect place to go when the hectic city pace has left you feeling tired. Regular Nose Hill visitors consider it Calgary's best-kept secret with its abundant flora and fauna and spectacular views.

From 14 Street NW, climb gradually on a paved path beside a coulee. In the fall, the colours on the hill are warm and inviting. Rich reds and burnt yellows are abundant in the coulees, where shrubs and aspen thrive. Leave that pavement and enter the dog walkers' mecca. The park has many on- and off-leash areas, so be prepared to meet a few furry friends. Back on the pavement heading south, enjoy views of Canada Olympic Park and the Rockies to the west, as well as Calgary's downtown office towers creeping over the horizon to the south. You can enjoy mountain

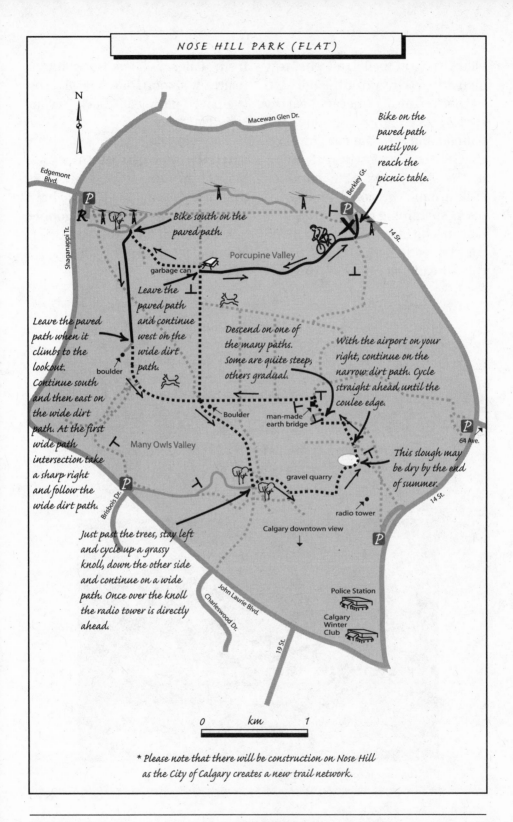

Macewan Glen Dr.

Berkley Gt.

Bike on the paved path until you reach the picnic table.

Edgemont Blvd.

Shaganappi Tr.

14 St.

Bike south on the paved path.

Porcupine Valley

garbage can

Leave the paved path and continue west on the wide dirt path.

Leave the paved path when it climbs to the lookout. Continue south and then east on the wide dirt path. At the first wide path intersection take a sharp right and follow the wide dirt path.

boulder

Descend on one of the many paths. Some are quite steep, others gradual.

With the airport on your right, continue on the narrow dirt path. Cycle straight ahead until the coulee edge.

Boulder

man-made earth bridge

Many Owls Valley

P

64 Ave.

This slough may be dry by the end of summer.

Brisbois Dr.

gravel quarry

radio tower

14 St.

Calgary downtown view

P

Just past the trees, stay left and cycle up a grassy knoll, down the other side and continue on a wide path. Once over the knoll the radio tower is directly ahead.

John Laurie Blvd.

Charleswood Dr.

19 St.

Police Station

Calgary Winter Club

0   km   1

* Please note that there will be construction on Nose Hill as the City of Calgary creates a new trail network.

views as you pedal all the way along the west side of the hill.

Back onto uneven earthy terrain; it's a bumpy ride along the plateau and into the old gravel pit that nature is slowly reclaiming. In the spring and early summer, cycle around the slough and watch ducks swimming in this rare water hole on the hill. As you pedal along the flat, wide paths on the top of the plateau, you can enjoy the view from Calgary's highest point. A relatively smooth downhill glide on the paved path leads back to your car on 14 Street NW.

Cautions/Highlights

Most of the route follows dirt trails that are bumpy and may have rocks and the occasional gopher hole. A mountain bike–style tire is essential for this route.

PRAIRIE CROCUS

In April, when the winter winds have warmed up, the purple-flowered prairie crocus is a welcome sign of spring. Often the snow is still on the ground when the crocuses emerge. They grow close to the ground so they can live through spring snowfalls and frosts. A member of the buttercup family, this fragile plant is more accurately named pasque flower. When the purple flowers die back later in the spring, a tuft of feathered seed structures takes their place. The fuzzy hairs on these tufts help the plant collect moisture and allow it to thrive in the dry prairie climate.

Keith and Oscar coast downhill through Nose Hill Park.

NOSE HILL PARK (HILLY), NW

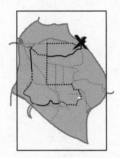

Categories: *nature, family, kids, non-stop, hill training, picnic*

Approximate Distance: *13 kilometres*

Terrain: *dirt path, paved path*

Degree of Difficulty: *moderate/difficult with some steep hill descents and long climbs on bumpy dirt trails*

Parking: *official parking at Berkley Gate and 14 Street NW intersection; or, official parking at Shaganappi Trail and Edgemont Boulevard NW intersection.*

Facilities: *bathrooms (on west side of park at Shaganappi Trail/Edgemont Boulevard parking lot), picnic tables*

Route at a Glance

With its panoramic views and isolated prairie landscape, Nose Hill Park is the place to go when you need to escape the rat race. This route begins with a slow, steady climb on a paved path, getting the blood pumping right off the bat. Leave that pavement and get ready to slow down and dodge an enthusiastic furry friend or two as you enter the dog walkers' mecca, an off-leash area. Views of snow-capped mountain peaks are a stunning springtime treat in this area of the park.

Back on the pavement heading south, look west for views of Canada Olympic Park and the Rockies. Calgary's downtown office towers are visible over the horizon to the south. The rest of the ride is on the uneven earthy terrain that mountain bikers love. The long descent on a single-track trail to the John Laurie Boulevard parking lot is a piece of cake for adept mountain bikers but a challenge for the neophyte. The climb that follows is a great workout as well as a popular spot to see white-trailed deer. Catch your breath at the top of the hill and then cycle over a grassy knoll into the old gravel pit. You'll soon encounter a slough that is full of water in the spring and early summer. Head into the park's interior, a wide open plateau. From spring through fall, the hill is alive with more than two hundred types of flowering plants. Strong winds that sweep the hilltop keep the mosquitoes away and cool you off at the end of your outing.

Cautions/Highlights

Most of the route consists of bumpy dirt trails that may have rocks and the occasional gopher hole. A mountain bike-style tire is essential for this route.

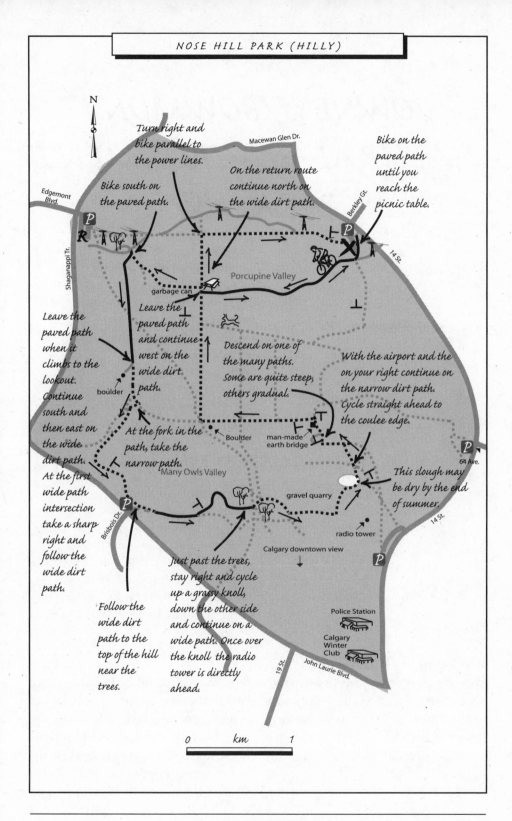

NOSE HILL PARK (HILLY)

N

Macewan Glen Dr.

Edgemont Blvd.

Shaganappi Tr.

Berkley Gt.

14 St.

Turn right and bike parallel to the power lines.

Bike south on the paved path.

On the return route continue north on the wide dirt path.

Bike on the paved path until you reach the picnic table.

Porcupine Valley

garbage can

Leave the paved path and continue west on the wide dirt path.

Descend on one of the many paths. Some are quite steep; others gradual.

With the airport and the on your right continue on the narrow dirt path. Cycle straight ahead to the coulee edge.

Leave the paved path when it climbs to the lookout. Continue south and then east on the wide dirt path. At the first wide path intersection take a sharp right and follow the wide dirt path.

boulder

At the fork in the path, take the narrow path.

Boulder

man-made earth bridge

Many Owls Valley

gravel quarry

This slough may be dry by the end of summer.

6A Ave.

Follow the wide dirt path to the top of the hill near the trees.

Brisbois Dr.

radio tower

Calgary downtown view

14 St.

Just past the trees, stay right and cycle up a grassy knoll, down the other side and continue on a wide path. Once over the knoll the radio tower is directly ahead.

Police Station

Calgary Winter Club

19 St.

John Laurie Blvd.

0   km   1

BOWNESS/BOWMONT NATURAL ENVIRONMENT PARK, NW

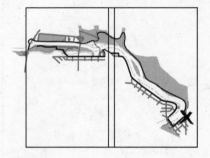

Categories: *neighbourhood, paved pathway, nature, family, bike trailer–friendly, kids, rollerblade, picnic, ice cream, lunch*
Approximate Distance: *15 kilometres*
Terrain: *quiet street, paved path, dirt path*
Degree of Difficulty: *easy and mostly flat with one long hill climb*
Parking: *Bowmont Natural Environment Park (east end): Park in the official parking area just off Home Road on 52 Street NW; rollerblade parking at Baker Park, 9333 Scenic Bow Road NW*
Facilities: *bathrooms at Bowness Park and Baker Park, playgrounds, water park at Bowness Park, picnic tables, firepits at Bowness Park*
Rollerblade Route: *Follow the Bow River pathway into Bowmont Park as far as you like before turning back. Bowmont Park has wide smooth trails and a couple of long hills.*
Ice Cream: *Angel's Drive Inn, corner of 47 Avenue and 85 Street NW (see sidebar); Leavitt's (Lics) Ice Cream Shop, 3410–3 Avenue NW (see sidebar)*

Route at a Glance

This route follows the quiet, tree-lined streets of Bowness. Bowness was a town in its own right long before it became a part of Calgary in 1964, and it has retained an independent culture and small-town feel. As you pedal along the route toward Bowness Park, the variety of original cottage-style homes, brand new big-city abodes, and hangover houses from the 1970s makes for entertaining commentary.

Bowness Park is the perfect spot to take the kids out of the trailer and stop for a play break in one of the many playgrounds. Mature poplars tower over the park and provide cool and shady relief in the summer. When the break is over, follow the paved Bow River Pathway past Baker Park and into Bowmont park, where the river views are stunning. The aspen archway next to the train tracks is a nice place to stop for a drink before embarking on the long hill climb. Pulling a child in a bike trailer up this hill is a leg-burning endeavour. Your efforts are rewarded, though, with Rocky Mountain views that make the climb to the top worthwhile. Continue along the wide, smooth path, which dips and climbs along the wildflower-covered hills of Bowmont park and offers views of the Bow River. On the last part of the trail, which runs along the river's edge, you can cool your toes in the cold waters of the Bow before you head off for an ice cream.

Cautions/Highlights

Bowness Park is very busy on summer weekends and evenings, so be prepared for a slow pace. Rollerbladers can enjoy the wide, smooth trails and long hills in Bowmont park. This is the perfect route for families with children in bike trailers or with older children who want to ride but need motivators such as ice cream, moving water, parks, and playgrounds to keep them pedalling.

LEAVITT'S (LICS) ICE CREAM SHOP

If you are heading east on Memorial Drive after the bike ride, be sure to stop at Lics. Not only an ice cream vendor, Lics also offers all the old-fashioned fast food delights: hamburgers and fries, hot dogs, and all sorts of fancy ways to indulge in an ice creamy treat. With more than fifty types of ice cream, sherbet, and sorbet, smoothies, milkshakes, and ice cream sundaes and splits, Lics is sure to please every member of your family. Decadent and delicious! Location: 3410–3 Avenue NW. Follow Memorial Drive (which becomes 3 Avenue) east and watch for Lics on the north side of Memorial Drive, just east of Shaganappi Trail.

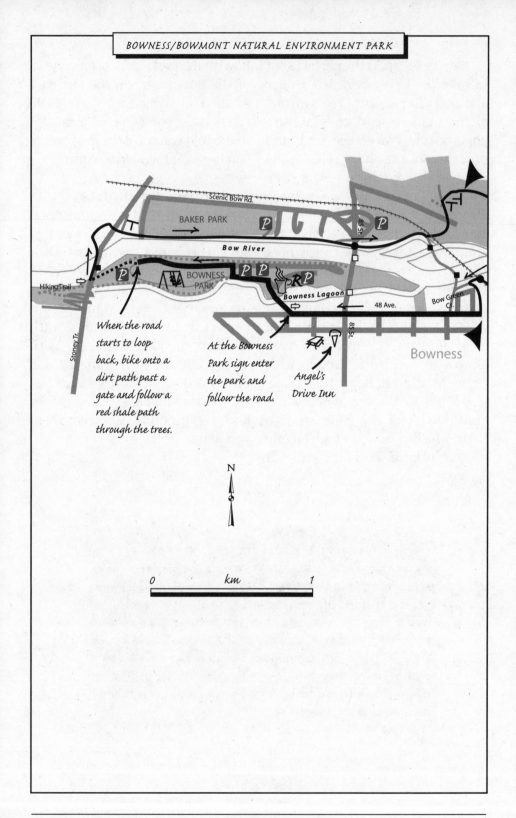

Scenic Bow Rd.

BAKER PARK

85 St.

Bow River

Hiking Trail

BOWNESS PARK

Bowness Lagoon

48 Ave.

Bow Green Cr.

85 St.

Stoney Tr.

Bowness

When the road starts to loop back, bike onto a dirt path past a gate and follow a red shale path through the trees.

At the Bowness Park sign enter the park and follow the road.

Angel's Drive Inn

N

0   km   1

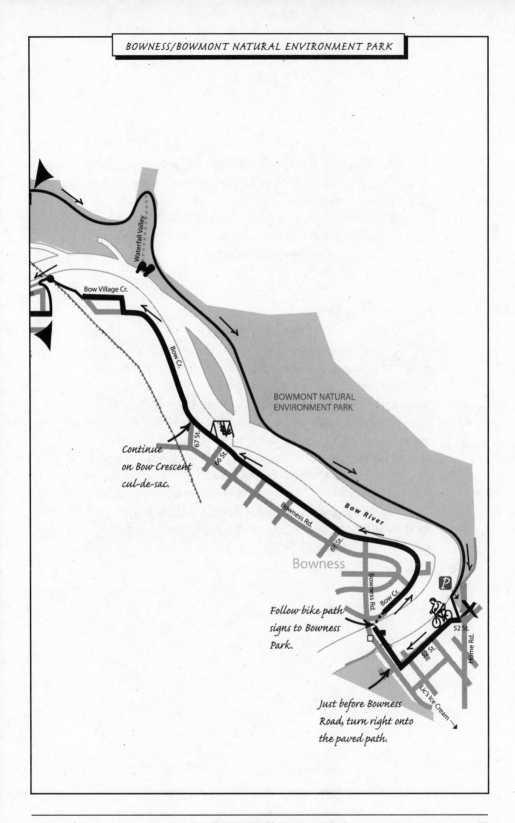

Waterfall Valley

Bow Village Cr.

Bow Cr.

67 St.

66 St.

*Continue
on Bow Crescent
cul-de-sac.*

BOWMONT NATURAL
ENVIRONMENT PARK

Bowness Rd.

69 St.

Bow River

Bowness

Bowness Rd.

Bow Cr.

*Follow bike path
signs to Bowness
Park.*

52 St.

52 St.

Home Rd.

Lic's Ice Cream

*Just before Bowness
Road, turn right onto
the paved path.*

ANGEL'S DRIVE INN RESTAURANT

Grab an ice cream, milkshake, or a burger and fries at this popular Bowness diner. You can sit at the picnic tables outside the restaurant or take your treats to Bowness Park and enjoy Bow River views while you indulge. Location: 8603–47 Avenue NW (corner of 47 Avenue and 85 Street NW)

CADENCE COFFEE

Stop along the Bowness shopping strip at this coffee shop with a diner feel. Enjoy a Power Breakfast of avocado, tomato, and egg on a Montreal-style bagel with fruit, or an omelette with all the fixings, before heading out on the trails. You can up the protein content of your meal by adding a Spolumbo sausage to any of the hot breakfasts. Muffins are baked from scratch in-house and are fresh daily and on the weekends, but homemade cinnamon buns are the baked good of choice. Hearty sandwiches are made on organic multi-grain breads from Heritage Breadworks, a local bakery. And if you need a little caffeine to start your day, the coffee is made from fair trade organic beans. Top-quality ingredients make this the perfect stop for a caloric top-up. Location: 6407 Bowness Road NW, phone: 247-9955

CONFEDERATION PARK/ NOSE HILL PARK, NW

Categories: *paved pathway, neighbourhood, nature, rollerblade, hill training, picnic, lunch, coffee shop*
Approximate Distance: *23 kilometres*
Terrain: *paved path, dirt path, quiet street, busy street*
Degree of Difficulty: *moderate with hills throughout*
Parking: *Confederation Park: Park on the west side of 10 Street NW in the official parking lot on 10 Street NW just north of 24 Avenue NW.*
Rollerblade Route: *Make a loop on the paved pathway that stretches east to the end of the Queen's Park Cemetery and west to North Capital Hill Park.*
Facilities: *bathrooms, playgrounds, picnic tables*

Route at a Glance

In May, after rain, Confederation Park is lush, green, and fresh. Paved paths make for easy riding past the tiny creek full of pollen. Slow down near the cattail-fringed wetland and listen for bird calls. Soon the golf course spreads out on the right, and bird calls are replaced with "oohs" and "ahhs" and the sounds of those hoping for birdies. The rolling path along the golf course warms up your leg muscles in preparation for the constant dip and climb throughout the ride. Continue on 19 Street NW, which is wide and easy to share with cars. The route soon meets a paved path in a green space that runs parallel to John Laurie Boulevard. This trail is a hidden treasure that hides the rider from the noise of the busy road above. Enjoy mountain viewpoints that offer a taste of what is to come once you reach Nose Hill Park.

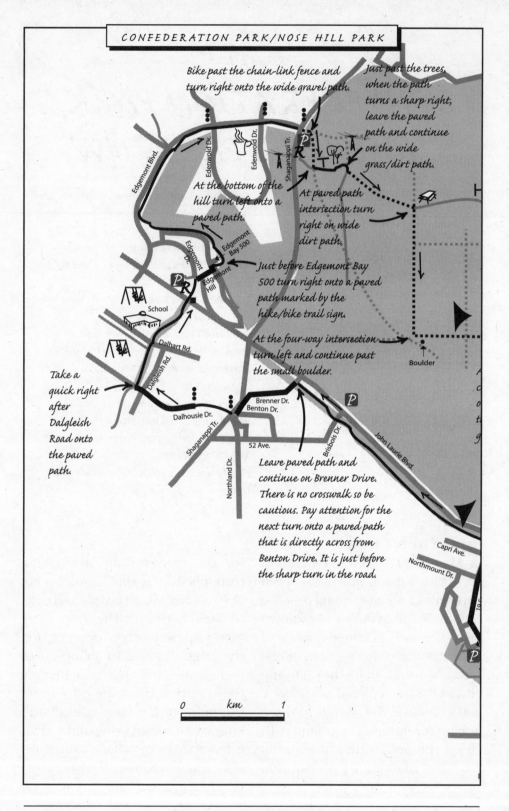

Bike past the chain-link fence and turn right onto the wide gravel path.

Just past the trees, when the path turns a sharp right, leave the paved path and continue on the wide grass/dirt path.

At the bottom of the hill turn left onto a paved path.

At paved path intersection turn right on wide dirt path.

Edenwold Dr.

Edenwold Dr.

Shaganappi Tr.

Edgemont Blvd.

Edgemont Bay 500

Edgemont Dr.

Edgemont Hill

Just before Edgemont Bay 500 turn right onto a paved path marked by the hike/bike trail sign.

At the four-way intersection turn left and continue past the small boulder.

Boulder

School

Dalhart Rd.

Dalgleish Rd.

Take a quick right after Dalgleish Road onto the paved path.

Dalhousie Dr.

Shaganappi Tr.

Brenner Dr.
Benton Dr.

Brisbois Dr.

52 Ave.

Northland Dr.

John Laurie Blvd.

Leave paved path and continue on Brenner Drive. There is no crosswalk so be cautious. Pay attention for the next turn onto a paved path that is directly across from Benton Drive. It is just before the sharp turn in the road.

Capri Ave.

Northmount Dr.

0   km   1

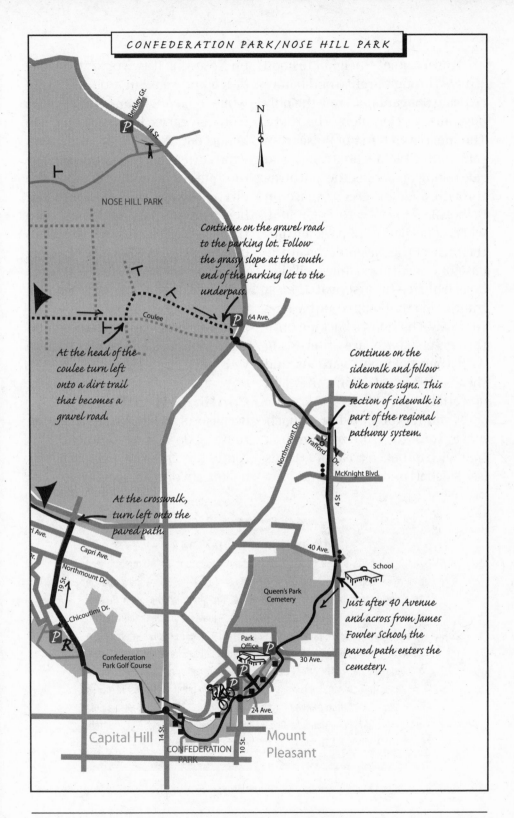

N

NOSE HILL PARK

Continue on the gravel road to the parking lot. Follow the grassy slope at the south end of the parking lot to the underpass.

Coulee

64 Ave.

At the head of the coulee turn left onto a dirt trail that becomes a gravel road.

Continue on the sidewalk and follow bike route signs. This section of sidewalk is part of the regional pathway system.

Northmount Dr.

Trafford Dr.

McKnight Blvd.

4 St.

At the crosswalk, turn left onto the paved path.

Capri Ave.

Capri Ave.

Northmount Dr.

19 St.

Chicoutimi Dr.

40 Ave.

School

Queen's Park Cemetery

Just after 40 Avenue and across from James Fowler School, the paved path enters the cemetery.

Confederation Park Golf Course

Park Office

30 Ave.

24 Ave.

Capital Hill

14 St.

CONFEDERATION PARK

10 St.

Mount Pleasant

Travel quiet neighbourhood streets through Brentwood before crossing Shaganappi Trail, the only busy intersection along the route. The short-lived burst of noise from cars and city life abates as you ride along a connector pathway through hidden green space in Dalhousie. Move on to Edgemont, where another mini-park awaits; then travel the paved paths at the base of a wildflower-filled hillside. Dogs run free here, so watch for a frantic Fido that may come barking your way. The homes backing onto this green space are interesting with their colourful gardens and shrubs. Then it's onward and upward to Nose Hill.

If you forgot to bring a snack, make sure to stop and grab a sandwich or baked treat at Friends (see sidebar) and have a picnic stop on Nose Hill. It is worth it to slow down and soak up a bit of nature while enjoying panoramic views from Calgary's highest point. On a hot day, Nose Hill's trademark winds offer cool relief and keep the mosquitoes away. Bump along the dirt pathways that lead into the heart of the park and then onto the paved paths through the parks of Thorncliff. A short stint along 4 Street NW leads to the Queen's Park Cemetery, where all is peaceful and quiet once again. Follow the pathway past playgrounds and grassy hillsides all the way back to your car.

Cautions/Highlights

Because of a few busy streets en route, I do not recommend this route for children or for adults pulling children in bike carriers.

FRIENDS CAPPUCCINO BAR

The homemade baked goods, sandwiches, and soups at Friends make it a perfect stop at any time of day. Muffins are baked fresh daily, and on Saturday mornings cinnamon buns come straight from the oven to your plate. Sandwiches are unique, made from top-quality ingredients and served on fresh-baked multi-grain bread. Try the Turkey Zinger on multi-grain with a touch of jalapeno jelly for bite. Grilled focaccia sandwiches come with sweet roasted peppers, warm brie, fresh tomatoes, and spinach. I love to savour a Crantastic Turkey sandwich while sitting on a high point on Nose Hill. If you need some caffeine to get you through the rest of the bike route, grab a coffee and perhaps a homemade dessert square to enjoy at the end of the trail. Location: 104–45 Edenwold Drive NW, phone: 241-5526

NOSE CREEK/WEST NOSE CREEK PARK, NE

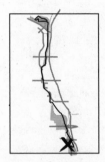

Categories: *paved pathway, family, bike trailer–friendly, kids, rollerblade, non-stop, picnic, ice cream, lunch, coffee shop*
Approximate Distance: *22 kilometres*
Terrain: *paved path*
Degree of Difficulty: *easy with gradual hills and one major hill climb that can be avoided*
Parking: *Just past the north parking lots for the zoo is an official parking lot on St. George's Drive NE for the Nose Creek Pathway; continue east past the zoo, down the hill to the parking lot on the right-hand side; or at West Nose Creek Park: official parking lot at the corner of Beddington Trail and Beddington Boulevard.*
Facilities: *year-round porta-potty bathrooms at the trailhead and at West Nose Creek Park, playgrounds, picnic tables*
Ice Cream: *Confetti Ice Cream: 4416–5 Street NE*

Route at a Glance

Planes and trains are your companions as you pedal along the paved paths that follow muddy Nose Creek. The Nose Creek Pathway is much quieter than the popular Bow River Pathway and so is perfect for parents pulling child carriers, for children riding solo, or for those who want to get on their bikes, choose their pace, and go for it. The relatively flat route follows paved paths throughout. A couple of sharp turns on hills and one breathtaking climb from the river valley to the escarpment edge are the challenges on this outing. The West Nose Creek Park trail system is a mix of bridges, gravel paths, and the paved bike path. Take a break on a bench at one of the pull-offs and enjoy views over the river valley, or read the interpretive signs offering historical tidbits about the sandstone quarried in this area.

Watch for the deer and coyotes that travel the natural corridor in West Nose Creek Park. The return route follows the same familiar path. Your post-ride treat could be an ice cream on a hot day, or a hot cup of coffee and lunch at the Riverside Coffee House.

Cautions/Highlights

This is the perfect route for riders who want to pedal non-stop, for those pulling kids in bike trailers, and for beginner cyclists and rollerbladers who want to avoid busy pathways.

HEARTLAND CAFÉ

What a treat it is to have the Heartland Café in Bridgeland! This locally owned café started out as a landmark in Kensington. The Bridgeland location is bright and spacious and chock full of tasty fresh food. Cookies the size of pizzas, a variety of muffins—including their trademark yoghurt raspberry, cinnamon buns with gooey icing, squares, brownies and my favourite, the raspberry scone. Go for a full breakfast, lunch, or dinner. Paninis, frittatas, grainy salads, and daily soups and specials; there is something for all tastes. This café is the perfect pit-stop post cycle or to charge you up before you head out. Heartland is open midweek from 8 AM to 8 PM and on weekends between 8 AM and 5 PM. Location: 116–7A Street NE, phone: 263-4567

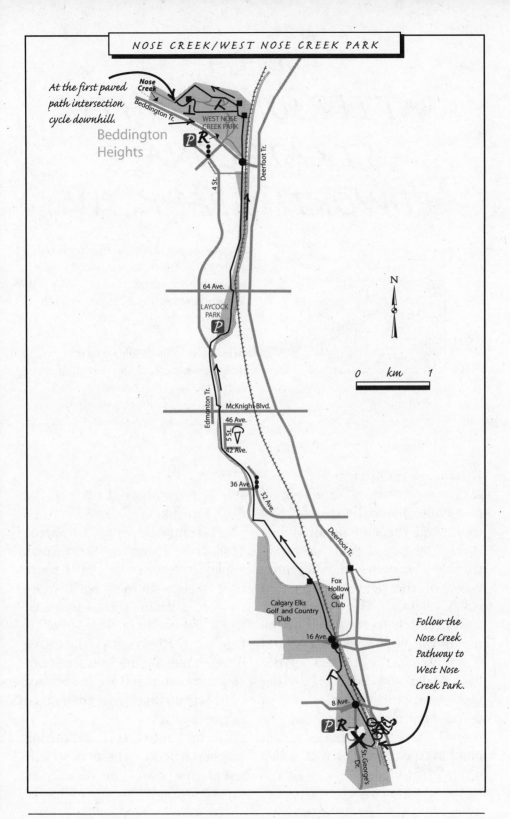

At the first paved path intersection cycle downhill.

Nose Creek

Beddington Tr.

WEST NOSE CREEK PARK

Beddington Heights

4 St.

Deerfoot Tr.

64 Ave.

LAYCOCK PARK

Edmonton Tr.

McKnight Blvd.

46 Ave.

5 St.

42 Ave.

36 Ave.

32 Ave.

N

0   km   1

Deerfoot Tr.

Fox Hollow Golf Club

Calgary Elks Golf and Country Club

16 Ave.

Follow the Nose Creek Pathway to West Nose Creek Park.

8 Ave.

St. George's Dr.

PATTERSON HEIGHTS/ STRATHCONA/ EDWORTHY PARK, SW

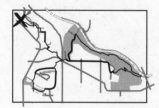

Categories: *paved pathway, neighbourhood, nature, culture, hill training, picnic, ice cream*
Distance: *15 kilometres*
Terrain: *paved path, quiet street, dirt path*
Degree of Difficulty: *moderate with lots of hills*
Parking: *Patterson Heights: park anywhere on the grass just off Patrick Street SW (a dirt road off Old Banff Coach Road)*
Facilities: *Edworthy Park: bathrooms, playgrounds, picnic tables, firepits*

Route at a Glance

A rural driveway and small farmhouse mark the start of this route and the end of all things rural. The paved path descends through aspen to sweeping views of the densely populated valley below. The impressive views stretch to Nose Hill in the north, the Bow River below, and downtown office towers to the east. Make note of the blinking CFCN television tower as it is a useful landmark throughout the ride. The tower site marks a high point in Calgary, and on a clear day offers great views. You can take a side trip on a paved path to the CFCN location.

Continue downhill to Sarcee Trail then climb to Strathcona. Poplar trees line the street route that passes homes with more character than those in most suburban neighbourhoods. Follow the steady climb with a dip into a heavily treed ravine. This short but sweet touch of nature leads back onto Strathcona Drive, then on to Edworthy Park.

Pedal into the Wildwood neighbourhood, where a speedy street ride takes you directly to the Quarry Road trail, a wide dirt path that descends through the trees to the Bow River Pathway. In late spring and early fall, watch for eagles soaring high above, or slow down and enjoy the colourful wildflowers that start blooming in May. The tiny blue violet is one of the first to add colour to the trail. In the fall, the full-leaf yellow balsam poplar and trembling aspen, dark-green Douglas fir and spruce, and rich red-osier dogwood foliage give a warm, cozy feel to this part of the trail. Leave the flat, smooth ride along the Bow River and start the cardio-intensive climb up Edworthy Street. Cross Sarcee and follow your breadcrumbs back to the car.

Cautions/Highlights

This is a very hilly route. Because the route involves some street riding, I do not recommend it for children or for adults pulling children in bike trailers. In the winter and spring, portions of the Bow River Pathway are covered with ice flows.

CANADA OLYMPIC PARK MOUNTAIN BIKING

If you are into single-track trails and enjoy the thrill of descending steep terrain, then visit Canada Olympic Park in the summer. Calgary's only full-service mountain bike park offers more than twenty-five kilometres of professionally maintained open and single-track cross-country trails. It also provides chairlift access to the top of the hill and boasts programs for all ages and ability levels. Those who like going fast can compete in race leagues for adults and children. Need more thrills? Adrenaline junkies can finish the day with a ride on the Road Rocket, a summer bobsleigh ride that reaches speeds of up to ninety-five kilometres per hour down the Olympic bobsleigh track. Hours of operation vary from May through to September. Call 247-5452 for current daily hill and season pass fees.

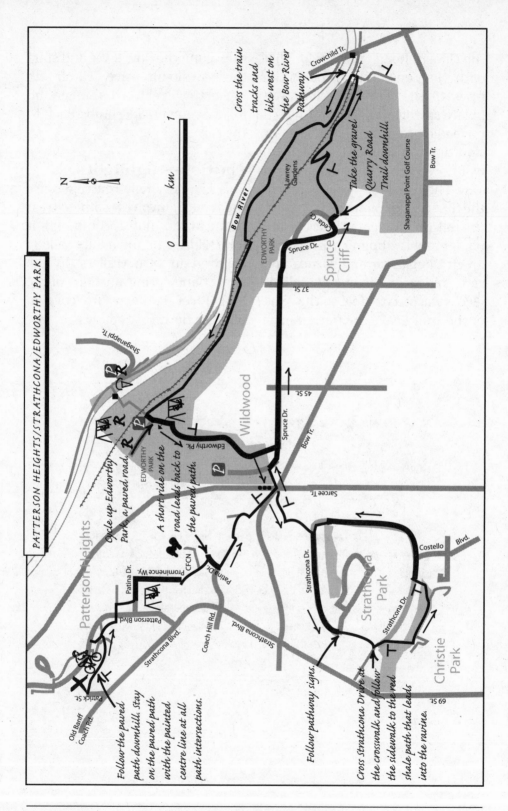

PATTERSON HEIGHTS/STRATHCONA/EDWORTHY PARK

Cross the train tracks and bike west on the Bow River Pathway.

Take the gravel Quarry Road Trail downhill.

Crowchild Tr.

Bow River

Lawrey Gardens

EDWORTHY PARK

Cedar Cr.

Spruce Dr.

Shaganappi Point Golf Course

Bow Tr.

37 St.

Spruce Cliff

Wildwood

45 St.

Spruce Dr.

Bow Tr.

Shaganappi Tr.

Cycle up Edworthy Park, a paved road.

EDWORTHY PARK

Edworthy Pk.

A short ride on the road leads back to the paved path.

Sarcee Tr.

Patterson Heights

Patina Dr.

Prominence Wy.

CFCN

Patina Dr.

Strathcona Dr.

Costello Blvd.

Patterson Blvd.

Strathcona Blvd.

Coach Hill Rd.

Strathcona Blvd.

Strathcona Park

Strathcona Dr.

Strathcona Dr.

Christie Park

69 St.

Patrick St.

Old Banff Coach Rd.

Follow the paved path downhill. Stay on the paved path with the painted centre line at all path intersections.

Follow pathway signs.

Cross Strathcona Drive at the crosswalk and follow the sidewalk to the red shale path that leads into the ravine.

0   km   1

N

WILDWOOD/ BRIDGELAND, SW/NW

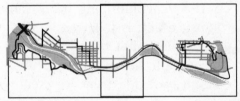

Categories: *paved pathway, neighbourhood, rollerblade, non-stop, hill training, picnic, ice cream, lunch, coffee shop (Riverside Coffee House: see Route 13 for details; Extreme Bean)*
Terrain: *quiet street, paved path*
Approximate Distance: *30 kilometres*
Degree of Difficulty: *moderate with one long gravel hill climb to Wildwood*
Parking: *Edworthy Park north parking area: At the intersection of Bowness Road and Shaganappi Trail, turn onto Montgomery View and continue to the parking areas; or, Edworthy Park south parking area: Follow 45 Street SW north of Bow Trail to Spruce Drive. Turn west and follow signs and winding gravel road to south side parking lot.*
Rollerblade route: *Follow the Bow River Pathway out and back for a flat paved-path route. There are several steep, on-street hills to negotiate on the bike path route into Bridgeland and Wildwood.*
Facilities: *bathrooms at Edworthy Park, picnic tables, firepits, playgrounds*
Ice Cream: *Moo's Country Ice Cream, Eau Claire Market; Leavitt's (Lics) Ice Cream Shop, 3410–3 Avenue NW (see Route 11 for details), Angel's Cappuccino and Ice Cream Café, 1111 Memorial Drive NW*

Route at a Glance

This route weaves in and out of quiet inner-city neighbourhoods, crosses one busy road, and returns on the paved Bow River Pathway before climbing a wide gravel path to the community of Wildwood and some great views. Start from Edworthy Park, then enter the neighbourhoods of Parkdale and West Hillhurst. This is a peaceful part of the route, as you ride under the cloak of full-grown trees. The Memorial Drive pedestrian overpass leads to the paved Bow River Pathway. This is a busy section of the popular pathway, so be prepared for bikes, rollerbladers, and pedestrians. Look to the left to see the Calgary Zoo's dinosaur prehistoric park and to the right for its new Destination Africa complexes.

Continue along the Nose Creek pathway and up the hill to Riverside. The views from Tom Campbell's Hill are worth a stop, and there are more views to come as the route continues through Bridgeland, a community of small, tidy homes on big, grassy lots. Carving evergreen topiaries is a popular pastime in the neighbourhood with the exception of one resident at the intersection of 8 Avenue and 9A Street NE. This home stands out for its impressive wildflower garden full of edible and medicinal plants. Even the green space that separates the road from the sidewalk has been planted with wild strawberries instead of grass. Around the next corner are breathtaking views of

Bridgeland below, the city core, and the mountains. A descent down a steep hill is followed by a peaceful pedal through Bridgeland and back to the Bow River Pathway.

Make your next stop Chinatown, Eau Claire Market, or Prince's Island Park, the site of several festivals and Shakespeare in the Park. Just west of Crowchild Trail, the paved route becomes a hidden oasis. The poplar trees are sticky sweet in spring and full of leafy greenery in summer. In late September, the shrubbery along the Bow River turns red, yellow, and orange, making it a photographer's dream.

The heart-pumping hill climb to Spruce Cliff is followed by flat, quiet streets that make pedalling a pleasure. In the summer months, enjoy a post-ride treat ice cream or cold drink at Angel's mobile concession on the north side of the river in Edworthy Park.

Cautions/Highlights
This route takes you to a couple of neighbourhood treats just off the central Bow River Pathway. Lots of hill climbs make this outing physically challenging.

EXTREME BEAN CAFÉ

Take a break at this little café that opened in the spring of 2003. Sit by the fireplace on a cool fall day or grab a slushy drink and head to the riverbank in the summer. Muffins are baked fresh daily, and lunch choices include sandwiches, mini-pizzas, and soup. Extreme Bean's convenient location along the Bow River Pathway makes it the perfect pedalling pit stop. Location: 3303–3 Avenue NW, phone: 283-6820

DOUGLAS FIR TRAIL

Lock up your bike at one of the racks provided at each end of this hiking trail and discover Calgary's best-kept secret. A combination of stairs, bridges, and dirt paths, the Douglas Fir Trail leads you through a rare stand of four-hundred-year-old Douglas fir trees. The trail is perfect for families and offers a change of scenery for dogs on leash. Wildflowers pepper the shaded route, while coyotes make their homes in dens in the escarpment. Great horned owls fly by at dusk, and woodpeckers rock their noggins throughout daylight hours. Why not bring a picnic for your post-hike treat? Edworthy Park has four playgrounds, covered camp kitchens, and open fire barbecues. Pick up a copy of *Calgary's Best Hikes and Walks* for a more detailed route description.

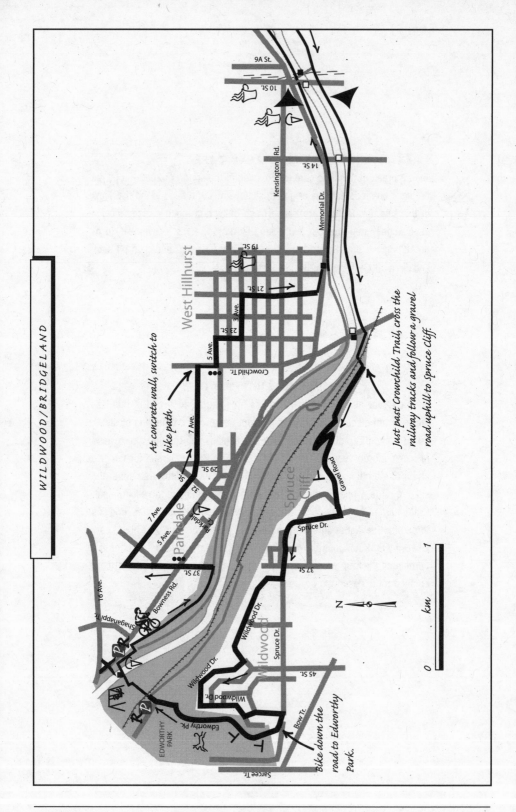

At concrete wall, switch to bike path

Just past Crowchild Trail, cross the railway tracks and follow a gravel road uphill to Spruce Cliff.

Bike down the road to Edworthy Park.

West Hillhurst

Spruce Cliff

Parkdale

Wildwood

EDWORTHY PARK

N

km

0   1

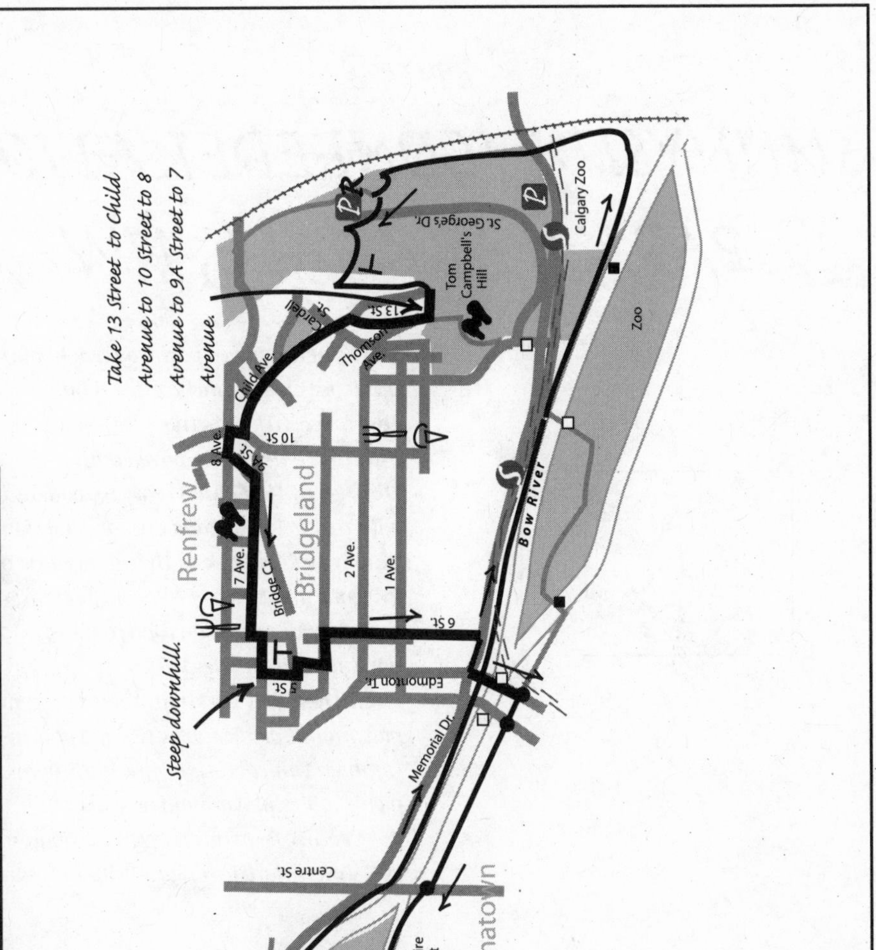

Rosedale

Renfrew

Bridgeland

Chinatown

Take 13 Street to Child Avenue to 10 Street to 8 Avenue to 9A Street to 7 Avenue.

steep downhill.

Bow River

Zoo

Calgary Zoo

Tom Campbell's Hill

St. George's Dr.

Thornton Ave.

Child Ave.

Randol St.

Bridge Cr.

13 St.

10 St.

9A St.

8 Ave.

7 Ave.

2 Ave.

1 Ave.

6 St.

5 St.

Edmonton Tr.

Memorial Dr.

Centre St.

Eau Claire Market

Water Park

YMCA

PRINCES ISLAND PARK

9A St.

10 St.

14 St.

Kensington Rd.

SUNNYSIDE/CONFEDERATION PARK/PARKDALE, NW

Categories: *paved pathway, neighbourhood, picnic, ice cream, lunch, coffee shop*
Distance: *20 kilometres*
Terrain: *quiet street, paved path*
Degree of Difficulty: *easy to moderate with rolling terrain and one long hill climb*
Parking: *Riley Park: At the intersection of 8 Avenue and 12 Street NW, continue east along the 8 Avenue extension road to the official parking area for Riley Park.*
Facilities: *Riley Park: bathrooms in summer, playground, picnic tables, wading pool in summer; Confederation Park: bathrooms, picnic tables, playgrounds*
Ice Cream: *Peppino's, 101, 1240 Kensington Road NW; Shivers Hard Ice Cream, 1840–20 Avenue NW*

Route at a Glance

The route starts with a pedal through the lush green grounds of Riley Park. This multi-use mini-park is a hive of activity in the summer. Manicured gardens, a large wading pool, huge playground, and lots of large poplar trees make it a nice picnic spot at the end of the ride.

Cycle through the park and follow the twists and turns of streets in Sunnyside, an eclectic, pedestrian-friendly neighbourhood. These streets lead to a paved-path climb up McHugh Bluff to views of the Rocky Mountains and the Bow River. The communities of Crescent Heights and Mount Pleasant are next on the route. Here you'll find homes that vary from early 1900s bungalows with tiny sheds to wallet-shrinking brand new abodes, and a few handyman's delights. A short stint on a busy street leads to the quiet, paved path in Queen's Park Cemetery and then on to Confederation Park, with its large

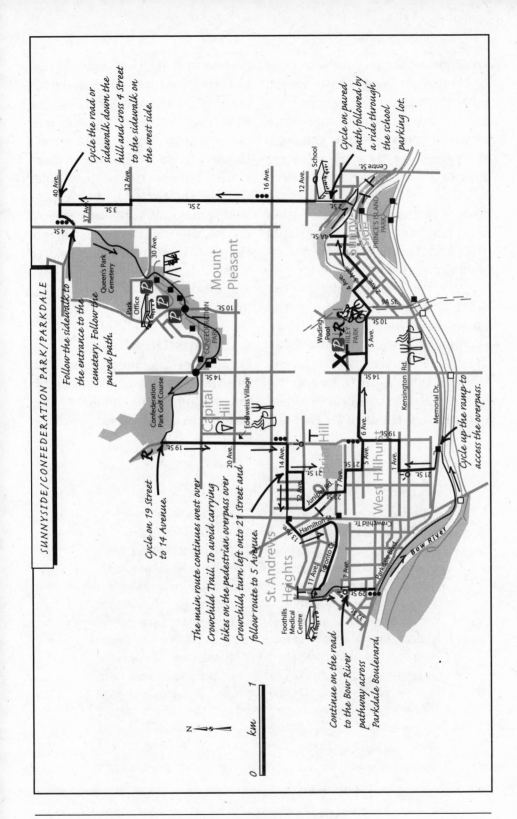

Cycle the road or sidewalk down the hill and cross 4 Street to the sidewalk on the west side.

Cycle on paved path followed by a ride through the school parking lot.

School

Follow the sidewalk to the entrance to the cemetery. Follow the paved path.

Cycle on 19 street to 14 Avenue.

The main route continues west over Crowchild Trail. To avoid carrying bikes on the pedestrian overpass over Crowchild, turn left onto 21 Street and follow route to 5 Avenue.

Cycle up the ramp to access the overpass.

Continue on the road to the Bow River pathway across Parkdale Boulevard.

40 Ave.
32 Ave.
16 Ave.
12 Ave.
37 Ave.
3 St.
2 St.
4 St.
Centre St.
2 St.
4A St.
Queen's Park Cemetery
30 Ave.
Park Office
Mount Pleasant
CONFEDERATION PARK
10 St.
14 St.
Confederation Park Golf Course
Capital Hill
Edelweiss Village
20 Ave.
14 Ave.
12 Ave.
Briar Hill
6 Ave.
5 Ave.
21 St.
7 Ave.
Juniper Rd.
22 St.
Hamilton St.
13 Ave.
Toronto Cr.
11 Ave.
7 Ave.
St. Andrews Heights
Foothills Medical Centre
32 St.
29 St.
Crowchild Tr.
Parkdale Blvd.
Bow River
West Hillhurst
1 Ave.
21 St.
19 St.
Kensington Rd.
Memorial Dr.
5 Ave.
14 St.
9A St.
10 St.
Wading Pool
RILEY PARK
5 Ave.
7 Ave.
9 Ave.
Sunnyside
PRINCE'S ISLAND PARK

N

km
0   1

Sunnyside/confederation Park/Parkdale   85

trees, grassy slopes, ponds, and lots of bridges crossing a fast-flowing creek. This is the perfect park for kids on bikes or on foot, evidence of which you will see as you cycle through. Soon the Confederation Park Golf Course comes into view, followed by a short ride on a somewhat busy street, a pedestrian overpass that crosses Crowchild Trail, and the fantastic views from St. Andrews Heights.

As you ride along the quiet street on the edge of the escarpment, look for a cluster of evergreens across the Bow River. This is Canada's most easterly stand of Douglas fir trees and the location of one of Calgary's finest nature hikes, the Douglas Fir Trail.

(See Route 15 sidebar for details.) Off the street and onto the paved path, descend into Parkdale and onto the Bow River Pathway. The section of the pathway is extremely busy; it's the only place on this route where I was almost run over. Soldier through the crowds to an overpass that leads to West Hillhurst; an ice cream shop and coffee stop are close by. A direct route leads back to Riley Park, where you can sit back and have a snack or cool your feet in the wading pool.

Cautions/Highlights

Because of the busy streets on this route, I do not recommend it for children or for adults pulling children in bike carriers.

EDELWEISS VILLAGE

Edelweiss Village is comprised of a café, a delicatessen, and a shop specializing in European imports and delicacies. This shop has every type of black licorice imaginable as well as some pretty fantastic chocolate. The café is a great place to stop mid-morning to fuel up on hot coffee and fresh-baked German-style goods. If you want something more substantial, try the home-made soups on a cool fall day or a hot meal of bratwurst and sauerkraut, pork or chicken schnitzel, or cabbage rolls. Jump up and down and shake all that food into one leg and then contemplate dessert. Try a slice of German torte with fresh cream, Tangerine Tango, German cheesecake, or choco-late-dipped marzipan cake, all of which will make your taste buds sing. It's no wonder the cafe is so busy at lunchtime! Post-feast pedalling might be a challenge, so plan on coasting down those hills. Location: 1921–20 Avenue NW; open 9:30 AM to 7 PM, Monday and Tuesday; 9:30 AM to 8 PM, Wednesday to Friday; Saturday from 9:30 AM to 6 PM; phone: 282-6600

PEPPINO'S RESTAURANT

This tiny lunch spot in Kensington offers twenty types of squash-proof baguette sandwiches, perfect for putting in a carry bag. You should eat one of Peppino's many flavours of homemade gelati, however, before getting back on your bike. Fresh pasta and a full selection of cheeses and other market items make this a tasty shopping stop. Location: 101, 1240 Kensington Road NW, phone: 283-5350

Late-summer snowfalls make gardening in Calgary a challenge.

INGLEWOOD/ MOUNT ROYAL/ SCOTSMAN'S HILL, SE/SW

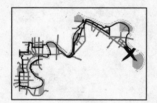

Categories: *paved pathway, neighbourhood, nature, family, bike trailer–friendly, kids, rollerblade, picnic, ice cream, lunch, coffee shop*
Approximate Distance: *20 kilometres*
Terrain: *quiet street, paved path*
Degree of Difficulty: *moderate with one challenging hill climb*
Parking: *Inglewood Bird Sanctuary: official parking lot near the end of 9 Avenue SE at Sanctuary Road*
Rollerblade Route: *Glide along this out-and-back route along the Elbow River Pathway and some quiet streets. Follow the Elbow River Pathway past Stanley Park to Riverdale and then backtrack along the same route.*
Facilities: *bathrooms at the Inglewood Bird Sanctuary when visitor centre is open: May long weekend to the October long weekend, Monday to Sunday, 10 AM to 5 PM; open in winter from Tuesday to Sunday, 10 AM to 4 PM; summer bathroom (Stanley Park), playgrounds, picnic tables*

Route at a Glance

The paved Bow River Pathway is the perfect warm-up for this inner-city route that climbs to hilltop views and glides along the lush, green river valley trails. The tree-lined Elbow River Pathway makes for a peaceful, pleasant pedal except during the second week of July, when the Calgary Exhibition and Stampede rolls into town. The "Biggest Outdoor Show on Earth" is Calgary's pride and joy. Watch for cowboys crossing

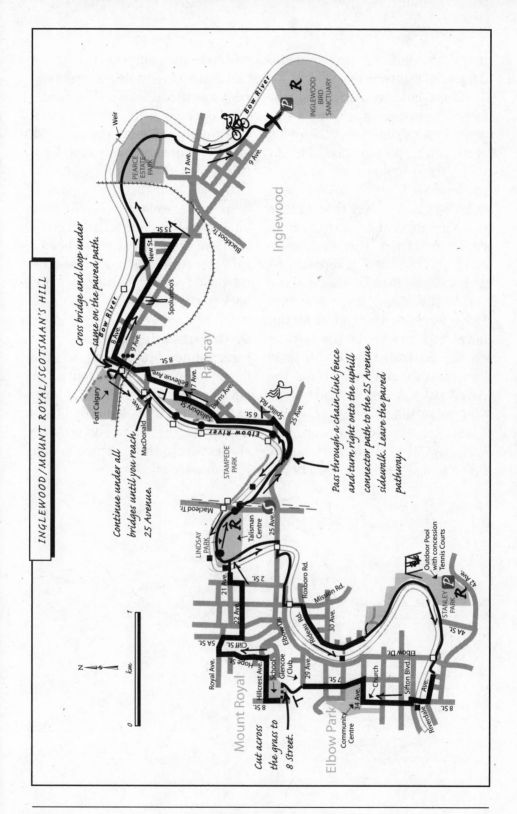

INGLEWOOD/MOUNT ROYAL/SCOTSMAN'S HILL

Cross bridge and loop under same on the paved path.

Weir

PEARCE ESTATE PARK

Bow River

17 Ave.

9 Ave.

Inglewood

INGLEWOOD BIRD SANCTUARY

Blackfoot Tr.

15 St.

New St.

Spolumbo's

Bow River

8 Ave.

9 Ave.

Continue under all bridges until you reach 25 Avenue.

Fort Calgary

Ave.

MacDonald

Ramsay

Bellevue Ave.

17 Ave.

Salisbury St.

Burns Ave.

8 St.

6 St.

Spiller Rd.

25 Ave.

Elbow River

STAMPEDE PARK

25 Ave.

Pass through a chain-link fence and turn right onto the uphill connector path to the 25 Avenue sidewalk. Leave the paved pathway.

Macleod Tr.

LINDSAY PARK

Talisman Centre

21 Ave.

2 St.

Roxboro Rd.

Mission Rd.

30 Ave.

Outdoor Pool with concession

Tennis Courts

42 Ave.

STANLEY PARK

4A St.

22 Ave.

5A St.

Royal Ave.

Cliff St.

Hope St.

School

Glencoe Club

Elbow Dr.

29 Ave.

Rideau Rd.

7 St.

Elbow Dr.

Sifton Blvd.

Mount Royal

Cut across the grass to 8 Street.

Hillcrest Ave.

8

Church

34 Ave.

Elbow Park Community Centre

Riverdale

Ave.

8 St.

N

km.

0   1

pathways and be prepared for detours at this time of year.

Cross Lindsay Park, past the large dome-top Talisman Centre, an ever-expanding sports complex, and enter picturesque Rideau, with its phenomenal summer gardens. Back on the paved path, enjoy a peaceful river ride under a tree canopy that leads to Stanley Park and then the impressive architecture of Riverdale. A pedestrian bridge takes you across the Elbow River and into Elbow Park. At the top of Mount Royal, enjoy views of the Rockies on the horizon before you head back toward Inglewood on the paved path. A detour leads up to Scotsman's Hill.

Soak up the views of Stampede Park and the mountains before descending past the pop-bottle stucco homes and tidy yards that make up this multi-generational neighbourhood. Some of the homes here date back to the late 1800s. The green grass and flowers of old-timers' properties contrast with the homes of the young and artsy with their landscaped rock gardens and stone walkways. Walk your bike along 9 Avenue SE if you enjoy window shopping or if you need a coffee or some lunch. Once back on the paved pathway, it's an easy ride back to the bird sanctuary.

Cautions/Highlights

I recommend travelling with a friend on any inner-city route. The paved paths along the Bow River in Inglewood and along the Elbow River near the Stampede grounds all the way to the Talisman Centre are quite secluded.

SPOLUMBO'S FINE FOODS

Dining at Spolumbo's is like hanging out with a bunch of jocks in suits. I suggest taking an aggressive stance in the lunchtime lineup. Hold your position and be firm with those who try to shove past you. This is full-contact sausage eating! Three former Calgary Stampeders football players who share Italian roots own Spolumbo's. Their meat-focused menu offers a variety of homemade sausages, from chicken and apple to spicy chorizo. Cycling non-carnivores can try the veggie subs. Grab a sandwich to go; any of their Italian meat and cheese choices are served on crusty buns. High chairs are available for those with babes in tow. Location: 1308–9 Avenue SE, phone: 264-6452

A springtime pedal past the budding trees in Mount Royal is a treat for the senses.

INGLEWOOD

Calgary's oldest neighbourbood is full of eclectic people and shops. In the commercial core on 9 Avenue SE, rejuvenated historic buildings house the city's largest collection of antique and home decorating shops. A scattering of coffee shops and ethnic eateries tempt taste buds, and the Hose and Hound Neighbourhood Pub (1030–9 Avenue SE) offers cold beer and burgers in a fire hall turned pub. If you prefer shopping to snacking, check out Recordland (1208–9 Avenue SE), where stacks of eight-track tapes and CDs share shelf-space, or Fair's Fair (907–9 Avenue SE), a used bookstore that fills up a warehouse. The back streets and alleys of Inglewood are home to wartime bungalows with car sheds and clotheslines. A refreshing contrast to Calgary's suburbs, Inglewood's mix of old and new is a joy to explore.

CAFFE ROSSO

Stop in at Caffe Rosso to fuel up and cool down. This coffee shop is a new addition in the community of Ramsay. Not far from the Stampede grounds, this café is tucked away in an up-and-coming area that is a work in progress in 2008. With its vibrant red walls and original artwork, it makes the perfect stop for the urban cyclist. Sip Italian imported Illy-brand coffees, sample the fresh baked goods, paninis and wraps, or grab a loaf of fresh bread to take home. Caffe Rosso is open midweek from 6 AM to 6 PM and on weekends between 8 AM and 5 PM. Location: 803-24 Avenue SE; phone: 479-2999

INGLEWOOD BIRD SANCTUARY/ CARBURN PARK, SE

Categories: *paved pathway, neighbourhood, nature, family, bike trailer–friendly, kids, rollerblade, non-stop, picnic, lunch*
Approximate Distance: *17 kilometres*
Terrain: *paved path*
Degree of Difficulty: *easy and mostly flat on paved paths with one hill in each direction*
Parking: *Inglewood Bird Sanctuary: official parking near the end of 9 Avenue SE at Sanctuary Road. The visitor centre is open from the May long weekend to the October long weekend, Monday to Sunday, 10 AM to 5 PM; open in winter from Tuesday to Sunday, 10 AM to 4 PM*
Facilities: *bathrooms (Inglewood Bird Sanctuary during visitor centre hours listed above, Beaver Dam Flats Park, Carburn Park), playgrounds, water parks, picnic tables, firepits*

Route at a Glance

Wheels start to roll and come to their final stop outside the Inglewood Bird Sanctuary. The 32-hectare wildlife reserve along the Bow River is a great place for a picnic lunch or supper after the ride. While enjoying a sandwich, you can watch for some of the more than 270 species of birds that visit the area throughout the year.

Industry and nature compete from the start of the route. The squeal of trains on tracks mixes with the jungle-like sounds of birdlife, and the drone of busy roads is constant. The Bow River Pathway leads to Refinery Park, Beaver Dam Flats Park, and Carburn Park, all reclaimed industrial sites, once owned by Esso, that now make up a single natural environment park. These areas teem with bird life, deer and coyotes. Walkers will enjoy the red shale paths along the river. In the wetland that sits at the bottom of the hill below Lynnwood, frogs croak their guttural songs. And speaking of croaking, take your time on the hill climb so you don't croak! After a gradual ascent, you'll be rewarded with spectacular views of the Bow River, downtown Calgary, and the Rocky Mountains. Descend into Carburn Park and loop around the lagoon before backtracking along the Bow River to the starting point.

Cautions/Highlights

Since the pathway is not cleared of snow in the winter, it can be icy in early spring.

Take a breather and soak up the views in Beaver Dam Flats Park.

INGLEWOOD WILDLANDS: FROM INDUSTRY TO NATURE

In 1939, a pipeline from Turner Valley transported oil to a refinery in Inglewood owned by British American. When Gulf Canada Resources purchased the refinery in 1971, it became an oil-storage and asphalt-production centre. Environmental controls were not as strict back then, and millions of litres of oil were spilled on the Inglewood Wildlands site. Chunks of asphalt could still be found there in 2003.

Hydrocarbons and traces of heavy metals contaminated the topsoil, and as early as 1977, oil slicks were spotted in the lagoon in the bird sanctuary. Cleanup began in 1979, after millions of litres of oil were discovered floating on the water table five feet beneath the surface. Workers pumped 400,000 litres of oil out from below the Inglewood Bird Sanctuary and Inglewood Wildlands that year. In 1985, Gulf closed the refinery and Petro-Canada acquired it as part of a parcel of lands.

Six years later, in 1991, the Rotary Club of Calgary suggested that the site be converted into a wildlands park. With monies raised by the club and donated by Petro-Canada, the conversion began. A pond was constructed on the site in hopes that birds from the sanctuary would visit. Ducks Unlimited provided the wetland vegetation, grasses, and wildflowers.

The long-term goal is to make Inglewood Wildlands an extension of the bird sanctuary. Native grasses have begun to take root, and bunches of wolf willow impart their sweet scent in the spring. Wild roses are calling the park home, and the cattail-ringed wetland makes a wonderful stopping point for red-winged blackbirds. Gophers live on the land along with coyotes and porcupines. Next time you bike by, make sure to stop and see for yourself the transformation from industry to nature. The land is coming back to life.

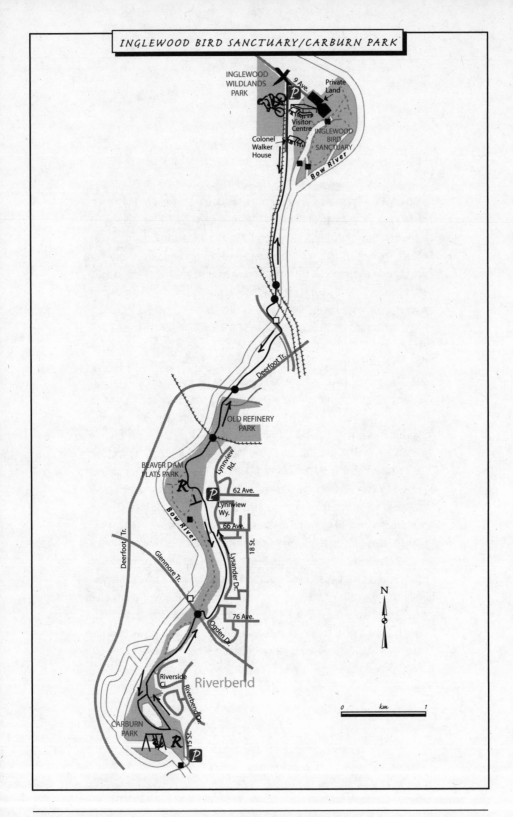

INGLEWOOD
WILDLANDS
PARK

9 Ave.

Private
Land

Visitor
Centre

INGLEWOOD
BIRD
SANCTUARY

Colonel
Walker
House

Bow River

Deerfoot Tr.

OLD REFINERY
PARK

BEAVER DAM
FLATS PARK

Lynnview Rd.

62 Ave.

Lynnview
Wy.

66 Ave.

Bow River

18 St.

Lysander Dr.

Deerfoot Tr.

Glenmore Tr.

76 Ave.

Ogden Dr.

Riverside
Ci.

Riverbend Dr.

Riverbend

15 St.

CARBURN
PARK

N

0   km   1

GARRISON WOODS/ MOUNT ROYAL/GLENMORE RESERVOIR, SW

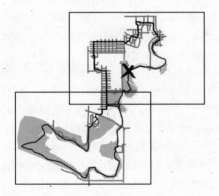

Categories: *paved pathway, neighbourhood, nature, family, bike trailer–friendly, kids, rollerblade, picnic, ice cream, lunch, coffee shop*
Approximate Distance: *Short Route: 14 kilometres; Long Route: 30 kilometres*
Terrain: *quiet street, paved path*
Degree of Difficulty: *Short Route: easy with one hill; Long Route: easy with two hills*
Parking: *Short Route: Garrison Woods, street parking outside My Favorite Ice Cream Shoppe at the corner of 42 Avenue and 20 Street SW; Long Route: South Glenmore Park, 90 Avenue and 24 Street SW; park near the playground and water park; Rollerblade Route: official parking at Sandy Beach. At the intersection of 50 Avenue and 14 Street SW, drive down the hill to the bottom and park near the playground.*
Rollerblade Route: *Follow the paved Elbow River Pathway from Sandy Beach, along Riverdale Avenue, past Stanley Park to Rideau Road. Continue along Rideau Road, cross the Elbow River, and follow the paved pathway along Elbow Drive. Take the next pedestrian bridge across the Elbow River and backtrack along the Elbow River paved pathway.*
Facilities: *bathrooms, playgrounds, water parks (long route), picnic tables, firepits*

Route at a Glance

Short route: Take the short route when pulling a young child in a bike trailer. It allows lots of time to stop at all the playgrounds, have snacks by the river, and even take a dip at the Stanley Park outdoor pool. Starting from My Favorite Ice Cream Shoppe, the route travels through a small portion of the impressive new community of Garrison Woods. Continue onward to South Calgary, where 1950s homes share space with new, high-priced infills. The gardens are fresh and fun in the summer, and for those of you with kids in tow, there is a fire station to stop at along the route, always a big hit with my young son. Soon the route leads into Mount Royal for a glimpse of some of Calgary's most impressive homes and gardens. The streets twist and turn to Lower Mount Royal and a possible detour to explore 17 Avenue SW. Soon the Elbow River Pathway leads into the Rideau neighbourhood and more striking homes.

The Elbow River Pathway is one of the most beautiful rides in the city. Enjoy towering poplar trees that line the streets and pathways, character homes and colourful gardens, and the peaceful flow of the river below. This area can be quite busy on warm summer evenings and on weekends, so plan a mid-week outing if you crave peace and quiet.

Follow the river through Riverdale to Sandy Beach and enjoy a long hill climb to River Park, where you switch to the Glenmore Pathway and head toward the Glenmore dam. Travel along the path at the escarpment edge and look down onto the vibrant green fairways of the exclusive Calgary Golf and Country Club. Soon the dam comes into view, your cue to head back to the car. Continue through Altadore to the ice cream shop just in the nick of time for your little ones!

Long route: Start near the Glenmore Sailing School on the paved Glenmore Pathway. To avoid the crowds, travel this route mid-week or early in the morning on summer weekends. A smooth, paved path leads downhill into the Weaselhead Flats Natural Area. The dirt pathways in the Weaselhead are wonderful for hiking but bikes are not allowed. Stick to the paved path and soon a hill climb leads to North Glenmore Park and wonderful views of the reservoir from the escarpment pathway. Travel through Lakeview and into Altadore, where you pick up the short route. Read the description above for details.

The long route starts up again from the reservoir dam. Cross over the dam and head back to the Glenmore Pathway along the reservoir. The mountain views are stunning from the east side of the reservoir. For a truly remarkable experience, plan to be there on a fall evening when the sun is setting and the mountains are backlit. Head to Glenmore Landing for a coffee and snack or continue along the reservoir pathway back to your car.

Cautions/Highlights

The short route is perfect for adults pulling children in bike trailers since there are lots of playgrounds along the way. It makes for a perfect half-day outing when stops are included.

GARRISON WOODS

Garrison Woods is a unique housing development situated on the former Canadian Forces Base (CFB) Calgary, also known as the Currie Barracks lands. This vibrant community was built to be pedestrian-, cyclist-, and transit-friendly. Its compact, pedestrian-scale developments offer shopping, services, and employment close to home.

Calgary is a city dominated by the private automobile. Because of zoning restrictions, very few suburban neighbourhoods have corner stores and handy shopping areas. This cuts down on diversity because only people who own cars can easily live in these residentially zoned neighbourhoods. That's why biking through Garrison Woods East is such a breath of fresh-air. It's a development that encourages diversity with its combination of housing types: single-family and semi-detached homes mixed with townhouses and apartment buildings.

Garrison Woods is a community with heart. People are out and about and I always end up chatting with someone while at the playground. Take a walk or ride through the area and watch its transformation. It's a recipe for success in creating a vibrant city!

CALGARY FARMER'S MARKET

Take a post-ride pit-stop at the Calgary Farmer's Market and fill up with fresh local fruits and vegetables. If you brought your panniers, you can stock up on locally raised chicken, duck, ostrich, turkey, eggs, beef, pork, elk, bison, and rabbit. Or simply indulge in the ethnically diverse selection of prepared foods that you can eat on the spot. The market makes a fun-filled stop for all ages. It is open year round on Friday and Saturday: 9 AM to 5 PM and on Sunday, 9 AM to 4 PM. In July and August it is open on Thursday: 9 AM to 5 PM (call to confirm); Location: H6, 4421 Quesnay Wood Drive, SW; phone: 244-4548.

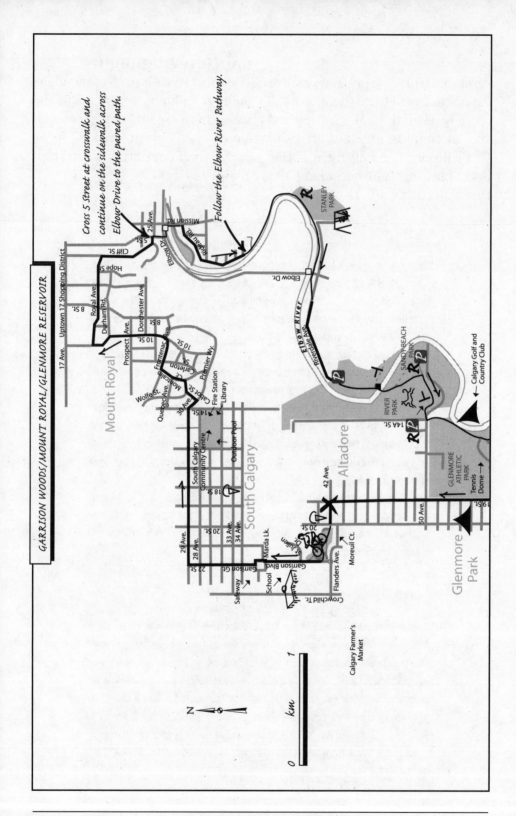

GARRISON WOODS/MOUNT ROYAL/GLENMORE RESERVOIR

Cross 5 Street at crosswalk and continue on the sidewalk across Elbow Drive to the paved path.

Follow the Elbow River Pathway.

Uptown 17 Shopping District

17 Ave.

Royal Ave.

8 St.

Durham Rd.

Prospect Ave.

Dorchester Ave.

10 St.

8 St.

Frontenac Ave.

Carleton St.

Premier Wy.

Montreal Ave.

Wolfe St.

Quebec Ave.

Gabet St.

30 St.

14 St.

Fire Station

Library

Mount Royal

25 Ave.

5 St.

Cliff St.

Hope St.

Elbow Dr.

Mission Rd.

Rideau Rd.

STANLEY PARK

Elbow Dr.

Elbow River

Riverdale Ave.

South Calgary

South Calgary Community Centre

Outdoor Pool

18 St.

20 St.

33 Ave.

34 Ave.

29 Ave.

28 Ave.

22 St.

Marda Lk.

Garrison Gt.

Garrison Blvd.

Safeway

School

42 Ave.

Altadore

20 St.

Flanders Ave.

Moreuil Ct.

Crowchild Tr.

50 Ave.

SANDY BEACH PARK

RIVER PARK

14A St.

Calgary Golf and Country Club

GLENMORE ATHLETIC PARK

Tennis Dome

19 St.

Glenmore Park

Calgary Farmer's Market

N

km

0   1

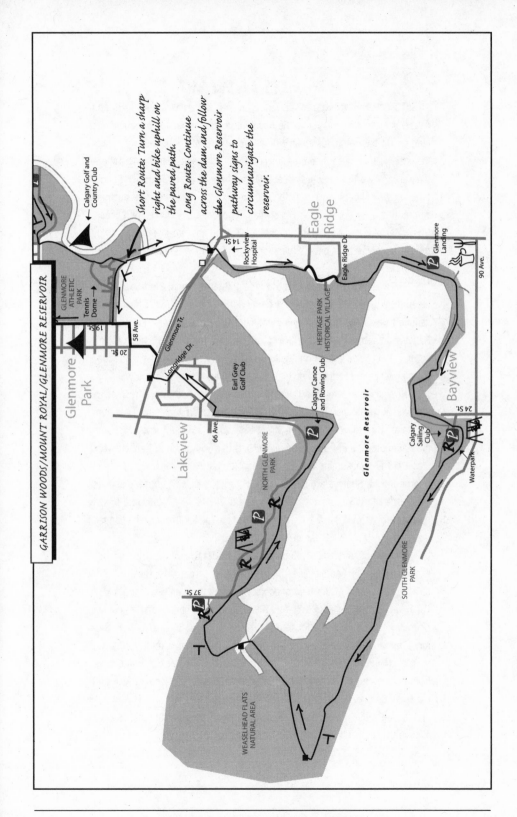

GARRISON WOODS/MOUNT ROYAL/GLENMORE RESERVOIR

Short Route: Turn a sharp right and bike uphill on the paved path.

Long Route: Continue across the dam and follow the Glenmore Reservoir pathway signs to circumnavigate the reservoir.

Calgary Golf and Country Club

Glenmore Park

GLENMORE ATHLETIC PARK

Tennis Dome

58 Ave.

20 St.
19 St.

Glenmore Tr.

Longridge Dr.

Lakeview

66 Ave.

Earl Grey Golf Club

NORTH GLENMORE PARK

14 St.

Rockyview Hospital

Eagle Ridge

Eagle Ridge Dr.

HERITAGE PARK HISTORICAL VILLAGE

Glenmore Landing

90 Ave.

Calgary Canoe and Rowing Club

Glenmore Reservoir

Bayview

24 St.

Calgary Sailing Club

Waterpark

37 St.

SOUTH GLENMORE PARK

WEASEL HEAD FLATS NATURAL AREA

UPTOWN 17 AVENUE SW

An urban cycling adventure can lead you through areas green, lush, and peaceful, or it can place you in the middle of a busy street, full of people and culture. On this route, leave your birding checklist at home and experience the latter: spend some time on 17 Avenue SW. This pedestrian-friendly shopping area is worth a detour and at least an hour of exploring. Spend some time window shopping (remember, you can't carry much with you because you're on a bike!) for wine, art, fresh-baked goods, funky clothes and shoes, CDs, specialty cheeses, and chocolates. During the warm months, enjoy people-watching on a patio while sipping a glass of wine and eating some cheap pasta.

Alternatively, you can design a lunch, shop by shop. Start with some bread from the Rustic Sourdough Bakery (1305–17 Avenue SW). Choose from various types of fresh bread along with cookies, cakes, loaves, and pastries. Regulars love the rye Berliner bread, but my favourites are the hearty five-, seven-, and twelve-grain breads. Be prepared to stand in line on a Saturday morning while regulars load up with bags of bread to last them the week.

Now make a detour north on 11 Street SW and grab some fresh salsa from the Mexican shop Boca Loca (1512–11 Street SW), then buy olives from the Kalamata Grocery (1421–11 Street SW). You'd probably never walk into the Kalamata Grocery unless someone had told you about it. Its well-worn storefront is unassuming and down-to-earth, just like its owners, Gus and George Kukos. Shelves are stacked full of Greek specialties but the sixteen types of fresh olives, four types of feta, and the variety of sesame-based halva are what will "make a Greek out of ya" as Gus told me after he handed me a spicy green olive to taste.

Back on 17 Avenue, continue east to 8 Street SW and visit the cheese experts at Janice Beaton Fine Cheese (1708–8 Street SW). Cleanse your palate with a taste of the best chocolate in the known universe at Bernard Callebaut (841–17 Avenue SW). And if you need a hot cuppa after a cool fall ride, stop in at Steeps Teahouse (Mount Royal Village, 880–16 Avenue SW) for a taste of their homemade authentic chai or peppermint chai. Choose from a variety of teas, from South African rooibos to black or white teas, from oolong and green tea to fruit infusion teas such as Coconut Kiss and Canadian Bonfire.

If you are heading home to make dinner, The Wine Shop (815A–17 Avenue SW) probably has the right wine for you.

MOUNT ROYAL/RIVER VALLEY/KNOB HILL, SW

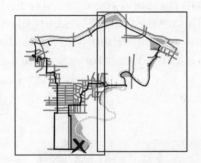

Categories: *bike pathway, neighbourhood, nature, culture, family, bike trailer–friendly, kids, rollerblade, hill training, picnic, ice cream, lunch, coffee shop*
Approximate Distance: *19 kilometres*
Terrain: *quiet street, paved path*
Degree of Difficulty: *moderate with a combination of easy paved-path riding at the beginning, followed by challenging hill climbs into the neighbourhoods of Shaganappi and South Calgary at the end of the route*
Parking: *River Park: official parking lot at the corner of 50 Avenue and 14A Street SW; Rollerblade Route Parking: Talisman Centre, 2225 Macleod Trail South (access parking on southbound Macleod Trail between 17 Avenue and 25 Avenue SE)*
Rollerblade Route: *Follow the paved Elbow River Pathway to the paved Bow River Pathway and continue as far as Crowchild Trail.*
Facilities: *playgrounds, bathrooms (porta-potties at the start, near the Pumphouse Theatre, and year-round inside at Eau Claire Market; outside in the summer at Eau Claire Market), picnic tables*
Ice Cream: *Moo's Country Ice Cream, Eau Claire Market; My Favorite Ice Cream Shoppe, 2048–42 Avenue SW; Confetti Ice Cream, 8, 2008–33 Avenue SW*

Route at a Glance

Cycle along a mix of paved paths and quiet streets, through architecturally interesting hilltop neighbourhoods with views of Nose Hill and the downtown core, past Stampede Park, and alongside

Chinatown and Eau Claire Market.

A ride past Mount Royal's grand abodes and landscaped yards is an inspiring start to this journey. Poplars shade the pathways and play host to chirpy songbirds that are in full chorus on early spring mornings. This route is full of hustle and bustle in the summer. The busy season starts during the second week of July, when you'll cycle past the hootin' and hollerin' Calgary Stampede grounds. Continue west on the Bow River Pathway and come to the Eau Claire Market and Prince's Island Park, festival central in the warm months. This is a great spot to slow down and people-watch while enjoying an ice cream. Continue along the flat Bow River Pathway past an art installation by the Stone Carvers Guild of Alberta,

then pass the Pumphouse Theatre before crossing the railroad tracks and climbing the first of many hills.

The first leg-burner takes you into Shaganappi, followed by Scarboro and Bankview. Hilly Bankview has a friendly feel with its mix of apartment complexes, wartime homes in their original state, and houses that have been fixed up by young urbanites. Enter South Calgary and bike through Marda Loop, the 33 Avenue SW shopping district. Take a ride along the avenue if you are in the need of brunch, ice cream, or a coffee. Then push on along the quiet streets of Altadore past neat 1950s bungalows. Slow down when you pass the Altadore Elementary School, one of a few city schools that have naturalized their schoolyards.

On a hot summer day, the tree-lined streets of Mount Royal provide shady relief.

There is something for everyone on this outing!

Cautions/Highlights

In the summer, neighbourhood gardens are spectacular. The portion of the route along the Elbow River near the Stampede Grounds is quite secluded while the Bow River Pathway can be very busy throughout the warm months.

CHINOOK GARDENING

As you cycle past colourful inner-city gardens, think about how much work goes into keeping plants alive and thriving in chinook country. We Calgarians welcome warm, dry chinook winds in the cold winter months, but our gardens are not as happy when the snow melts in January, exposing them to winter's bite. Plants exposed to chinook winds start the processes needed to grow new root hairs and open leaf and flower buds too early, and then become vulnerable to cold and frost because they can't return to their previous state of growth. Calgary gardeners work hard to keep their plants hibernating until June, when it is safe to assume that summer has arrived. The unveiling of plants brings a whirlwind of colour to the city that lasts until the next frost in September. Get out there and soak up the colour before the hibernation begins.

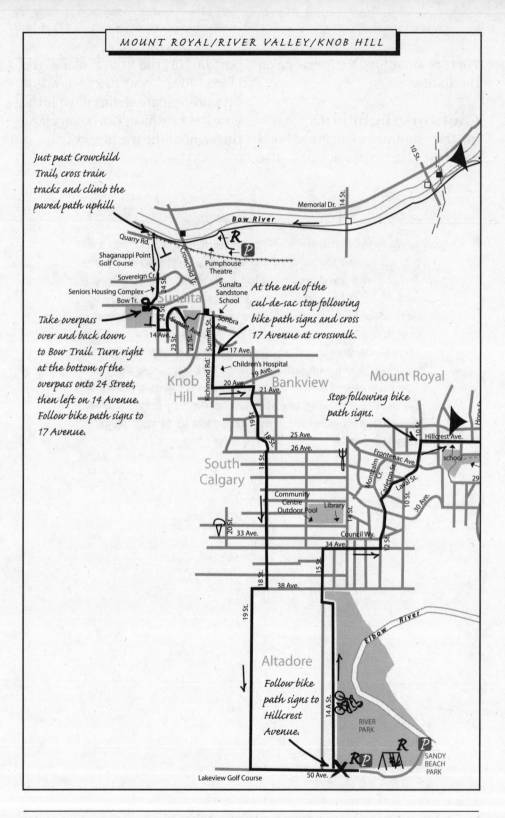

Just past Crowchild Trail, cross train tracks and climb the paved path uphill.

Quarry Rd.

Shaganappi Point Golf Course

Sovereign Cr.

Seniors Housing Complex
Bow Tr.

Take overpass over and back down to Bow Trail. Turn right at the bottom of the overpass onto 24 Street, then left on 14 Avenue. Follow bike path signs to 17 Avenue.

Pumphouse Theatre

Sunalta Sandstone School

Sunalta

14 Ave.

Sonora Ave.

At the end of the cul-de-sac stop following bike path signs and cross 17 Avenue at crosswalk.

17 Ave.

Children's Hospital
19 Ave.
20 Ave.
21 Ave.

Knob Hill

Bankview

Mount Royal

stop following bike path signs.

Hillcrest Ave.

school

25 Ave.
26 Ave.

Frontenac Ave.

South Calgary

Montcalm Cr.

Carleton St.

Laval St.

Community Centre
Outdoor Pool

Library

Council Wy.

33 Ave.

34 Ave.

38 Ave.

Altadore

Follow bike path signs to Hillcrest Avenue.

Elbow River

River Park

Sandy Beach Park

Lakeview Golf Course

50 Ave.

Bow River

Memorial Dr.

10 St.

14 St.

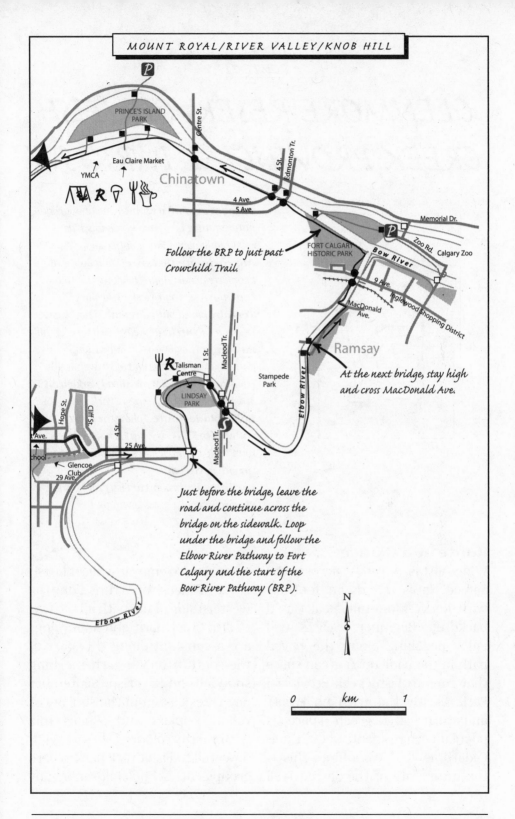

Follow the BRP to just past Crowchild Trail.

At the next bridge, stay high and cross MacDonald Ave.

Just before the bridge, leave the road and continue across the bridge on the sidewalk. Loop under the bridge and follow the Elbow River Pathway to Fort Calgary and the start of the Bow River Pathway (BRP).

GLENMORE RESERVOIR/FISH CREEK PROVINCIAL PARK, SW

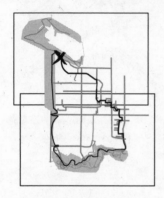

Categories: *paved pathway, neighbourhood, nature, family, bike trailer–friendly, kids, rollerblade, picnic, lunch, coffee shop*
Approximate Distance: *Long Route: 20 kilometres; Short Route: 11 kilometres round trip from reservoir to Fish Creek park*
Terrain: *paved path, dirt path, quiet street*
Degree of Difficulty: *easy with very few hills*
Parking: *official Weaselhead parking: parking area "B" at the end of 90 Avenue SW; Long Route: official Weaselhead parking off 37 Street SW in North Glenmore Park*
Rollerblade Route: *Follow the paved pathway to Fish Creek park. This 11-kilometre round-trip outing follows a mostly flat and smooth paved path.*
Facilities: *bathrooms at Fish Creek park, playgrounds, picnic tables, firepits*

Route at a Glance

Wide vistas stretch across the Sarcee Native Lands to foothills with Rocky Mountain peaks as a backdrop. Beginner cyclists will enjoy pedalling along the paved path in the wide open green space that runs to Fish Creek Provincial Park. Mostly flat with no twists and turns, the green space is popular with residents of Oakridge, Cedarbrae, and Woodbine. This is the future site of the Sarcee Trail

extension, so enjoy it while it lasts!

An off-leash area runs along the western side of the path all the way to Fish Creek park, and happy dogs are a constant along this part of the route. After an early-morning snowfall on a crisp September day, trees glisten in the sun. Burnt yellow poplars and aspens mix with earthy coloured shrubs. Wind downhill to Fish Creek park, where groups of schoolchildren enjoy experiential learning days at the Shannon Terrace Environmental Learning Centre. Pet the horses at the Shannon Terrace stables before continuing along the forested paved path. A cozy tree canopy shades the path until the next parking area, called Bebo Grove. Just past Bebo Grove, enter a prairie grass meadow that hosts vibrant earthy hues in September and October. Enjoy the hillside reds, oranges, and yellows before dipping into the trees and crossing the first bridge over Fish Creek. You'll criss-cross the creek a few times before leaving the park at Votier's Flats.

Once across Canyon Meadows Drive, the route follows the signed bike route along quiet streets. Two walkway overpasses allow you to move along without many stops at busy intersections. A peaceful pedal along the streets of Oakridge is the perfect way to finish your ride.

Cautions/Highlights

The smooth, flat path from the reservoir to Fish Creek is perfect for beginner cyclists testing their skills.

PATISSERIE DU SOLEIL

This little bakery in Glenmore Landing Shopping Centre is a great place to build a picnic lunch that you can enjoy en route. Try a vegetarian, chicken, beef, or spicy beef Jamaican patty, or a ham and cheese croissant. For a sweet snack, try a cinnamon bun or one of the many types of fruit tarts. You can also grab a loaf of homemade bread, head to Safeway for some cheese and fruit, and enjoy a European-style picnic lunch. Location: Glenmore Landing Shopping Centre, 147C, 1600–90 Avenue SW

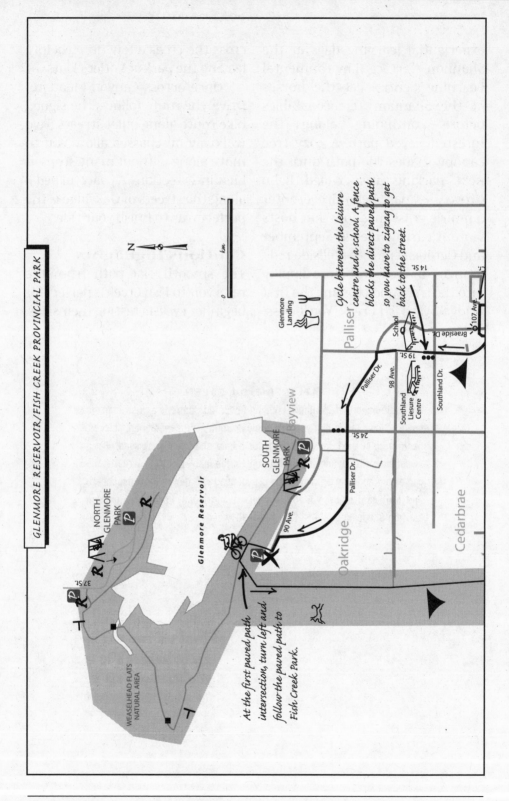

GLENMORE RESERVOIR/FISH CREEK PROVINCIAL PARK

N

0   1
        km.

Glenmore Landing

Palliser

Cycle between the leisure centre and a school. A fence blocks the direct paved path so you have to zigzag to get back to the street.

14 St.

School

19 St.

Braeside Dr.

107 Ave.

Palliser Dr.

98 Ave.

Southland Liesure Centre

Southland Dr.

24 St.

Bayview

SOUTH GLENMORE PARK

Palliser Dr.

90 Ave.

Oakridge

Cedarbrae

NORTH GLENMORE PARK

37 St.

Glenmore Reservoir

WEASELHEAD FLATS NATURAL AREA

At the first paved path intersection, turn left and follow the paved path to Fish Creek Park.

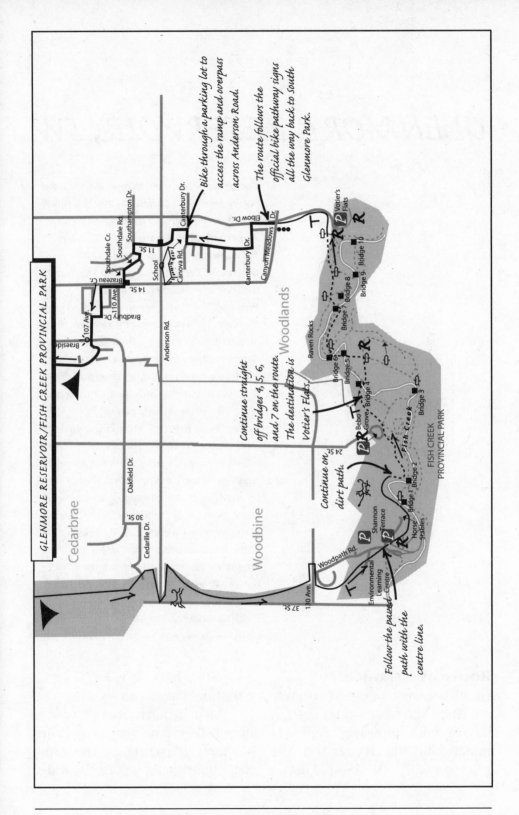

GLENMORE RESERVOIR/FISH CREEK PROVINCIAL PARK

Bike through a parking lot to access the ramp and overpass across Anderson Road.

The route follows the official bike pathway signs all the way back to South Glenmore Park.

Continue straight off bridges 4, 5, 6, and 7 on the route. The destination is Votier's Flats.

Continue on dirt path

Follow the paved path with the centre line.

Cedarbrae

Woodbine

Woodlands

FISH CREEK PROVINCIAL PARK

GLENMORE RESERVOIR, SW

Categories: *paved pathway, neighbourhood, nature, family, bike trailer–friendly, kids, rollerblade, non-stop, picnic, ice cream, lunch, coffee shop*

Approximate Distance: *16.5 kilometres*

Terrain: *paved path, quiet street*

Degree of Difficulty: *easy and mostly flat with one long descent and hill climb*

Parking: *There are many official parking lots on the north and south sides of the reservoir. Here are a couple of options: South Glenmore Park: at the intersection of 90 Avenue and 24 Street SW; North Glenmore Park: Follow Crowchild Trail or 37 Street SW south to North Glenmore Park and park at any of the "lettered" parking lots.*

Rollerblade Route: *The parking options and route are the same as for the bike route. Please be aware that just west of South Glenmore Park is a steep hill with a sharp turn at the bottom followed by a bridge crossing. Accidents, some of them resulting in head injuries, are common at this location. Unless you are extremely proficient on rollerblades, avoid this hill.*

Facilities: *year-round bathrooms at the Weaselhead parking lot, just past the Rockyview Hospital; summer bathrooms in North Glenmore and South Glenmore Parks, playgrounds, water parks, picnic tables, firepits*

Route at a Glance

For all the west- and east-coasters out there, the reservoir is Calgary's largest body of water. Sailboats moving in the breeze on the reservoir will remind you of home, if without the sea air.

Much of this route follows the paved Glenmore Pathway, with a short ride through the quiet neighbourhoods of Eagle Ridge

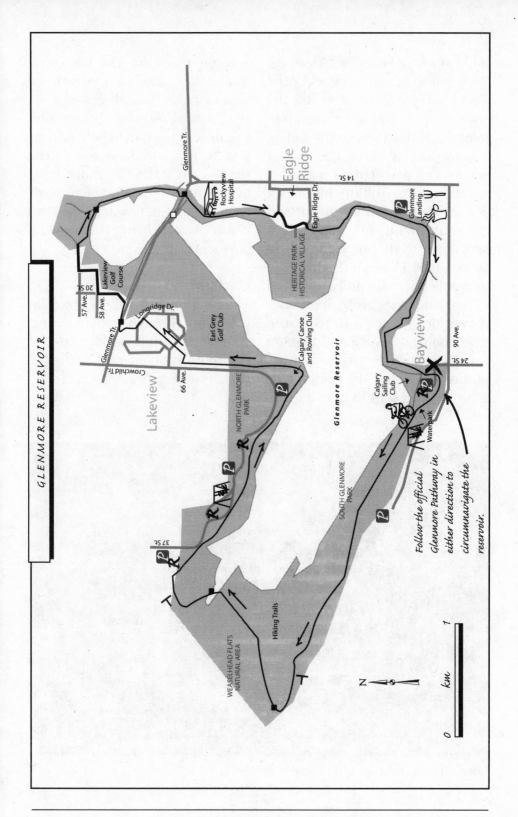

GLENMORE RESERVOIR

Glenmore Tr.

Rockyview Hospital

Eagle Ridge

14 St.

Eagle Ridge Dr.

HERITAGE PARK HISTORICAL VILLAGE

Glenmore Landing

20 St.

57 Ave.

58 Ave.

Lakeview Golf Course

Longridge Dr.

Glenmore Tr.

Crowchild Tr.

66 Ave.

Earl Grey Golf Club

Calgary Canoe and Rowing Club

Glenmore Reservoir

Bayview

90 Ave.

24 St.

Calgary Sailing Club

Lakeview

NORTH GLENMORE PARK

Waterpark

SOUTH GLENMORE PARK

37 St.

Follow the official Glenmore Pathway in either direction to circumnavigate the reservoir.

WEASELHEAD FLATS NATURAL AREA

Hiking Trails

N

0   km   1

and Lakeview. Pedal past Heritage Park and soak up the views of the Rockies on the horizon. In the spring, the cocktail party sounds of inland gulls lead you to the sailing school. Just west of the sailing school, the path enters a shaded aspen archway full of chickadees. These friendly birds love to land on your hands for a snack of sunflower seeds. Down the hill, in Weaselhead Flats, you'll cross the Beaver Pond bridge and a pond full of croaking frogs, geese, and ducks. If you long to see a beaver, stop near the next bridge and look up the Elbow River. I often see beavers at dusk just below the bridge. This is also a good spot to have a drink and get ready for the hill climb that takes you to magnificent views of the Weaselhead against the backdrop of mountains. Organize a personal chef to meet you for a barbecue at one of the firepits in North Glenmore Park. Make sure to book that picnic spot with the City of Calgary (268-3830) if you plan on being there in the busy summer season.

Cautions/Highlights

The reservoir route is very busy on weekends throughout the spring, summer, and fall. Luckily, part of the route has separate paths for walkers and cyclists.

Sailboats prepare to launch on the Glenmore Reservoir.

CARBURN PARK/ DOUGLASDALE/FISH CREEK PROVINCIAL PARK, SE

Categories: *paved pathway, nature, family, bike trailer–friendly, kids, rollerblade, non-stop, picnic, ice cream (summer), lunch (summer)*
Approximate Distance: *17 kilometres*
Terrain: *paved path, shale path*
Degree of Difficulty: *easy with mostly flat terrain and one major hill climb.*
Parking: *official parking at Carburn Park, 8925–15 Street SE*
Facilities: *bathrooms, playgrounds, picnic tables, firepits*

Route at a Glance

It's hard to believe that Carburn Park, with its picturesque lake surrounded by forest and the Bow River, was once the site of the Burnco gravel pit. It's a good example of how people can bring nature back when industry has moved on. The flat start to this route is the perfect warm-up for the hill climbing to come. Follow the Bow River Pathway to the northernmost tip of Fish Creek Provincial Park, where the climb up the escarpment leads to wonderful views of the Bow River, Fish Creek park, and the mountains. The paved path rolls gently at times but is mostly flat, perfect for new cyclists. The steep switchback descent to Fish Creek Provincial Park leads to a bridge over the Bow River. Take a detour south to Sikome Lake in the summer for a dip and a snack. Another interesting detour is the Bow Valley Ranch interpretive centre, where you can learn more about the park's 8,000-year-old human history. This new archaeological area includes a range of interactive displays and a working laboratory, giving visitors a chance to view ancient and historical artifacts that have been excavated from sites throughout the park. After these exciting detours, head east on the paved path all the way back to Carburn Park.

Cautions/Highlights

This mostly flat paved-path route is perfect for beginner cyclists. One hill climb and descent adds a cardiovascular challenge.

ARCHAEOLOGY IN FISH CREEK PROVINCIAL PARK

Stop in at the Bow Valley Ranch information centre and learn about the archaeological sites in Fish Creek park. Humans are believed to have first settled in small numbers in the Fish Creek Valley around 6000 BC. The University of Calgary archaeological team has uncovered more than seventy sites in the valley, as well as evidence of early buffalo hunts (750 BC–1700 AD), native weaponry, cooking utensils, and other ancient artifacts. The oldest identifiable artifact found in the park so far is a broken spearhead, thought to be from around 2500 BC. Your children might enjoy the public digs that the archaeological interpretative centre offers throughout the summer. Call 271-6333 to find out more.

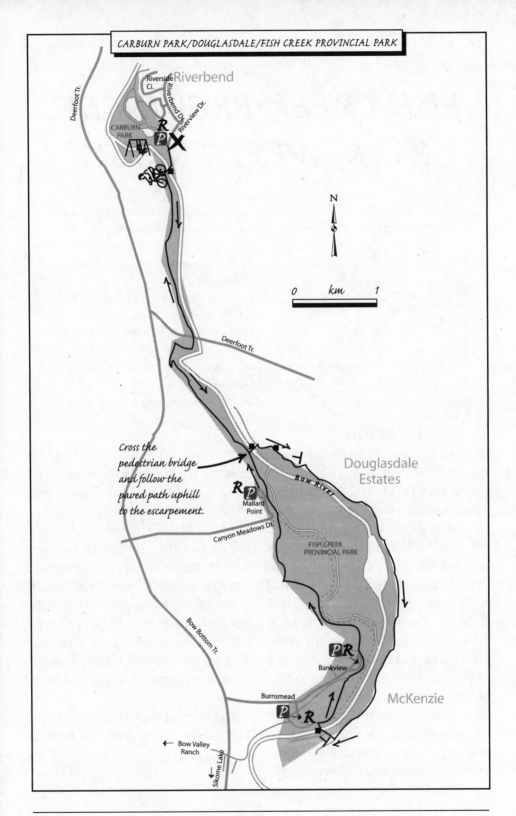

Cross the pedestrian bridge and follow the paved path uphill to the escarpement.

FISH CREEK PROVINCIAL PARK, WEST END, SW

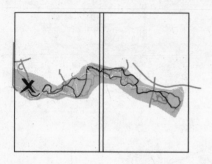

Categories: *paved pathway, nature, culture, family, bike trailer–friendly, kids, non-stop, picnic*
Approximate Distance: *16 kilometres*
Terrain: *paved path, shale path*
Degree of Difficulty: *easy and mostly flat with one hill climb*
Parking: *Shannon Terrace: From 130 Avenue SW turn south onto Woodpath Road to enter Fish Creek park. Stay straight on this road until you come to a Y intersection. Keep to the left and continue to the first parking lot near the bathrooms.*
Facilities: *bathrooms, picnic tables, firepits*

Route at a Glance

This shady route travels on paved and red shale paths through forests along Fish Creek. Pedal through a re-energizing oasis of nature that is wonderful year-round but is especially colourful in the summer and fall, when the trees and shrubs are in full leaf. In August, ripened saskatoon berries will tempt cyclists to slow down for a taste. Lots of twists and turns lead off the main bike route and take riders into the heart of the park. Plan on riding slowly and making many stops. Kids love this route for its variety of scenery and for the chance to stick their fingers and feet in the creek. Combine rock-throwing stops with snack time, and watch for the resident mule deer in the trees or the great horned owls that enjoy sitting in the bare branches of balsam poplars. At the turnaround point, the topography changes from treed canopy to wide open grasslands. Unpack your picnic lunch at one of many picnic tables along the route before looping back for fresh views and a chance to meet the Shannon Terrace trail horses if they happen to be hanging out near the pathway.

Cautions/Highlights

This route is nice and shady on a hot summer day.

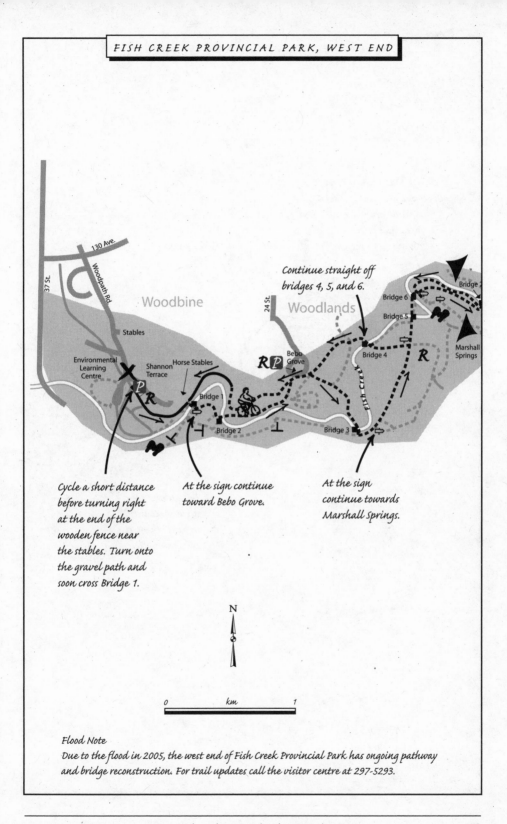

Cycle a short distance before turning right at the end of the wooden fence near the stables. Turn onto the gravel path and soon cross Bridge 1.

At the sign continue toward Bebo Grove.

At the sign continue towards Marshall Springs.

Continue straight off bridges 4, 5, and 6.

N

0   km   1

Flood Note
Due to the flood in 2005, the west end of Fish Creek Provincial Park has ongoing pathway and bridge reconstruction. For trail updates call the visitor centre at 297-5293.

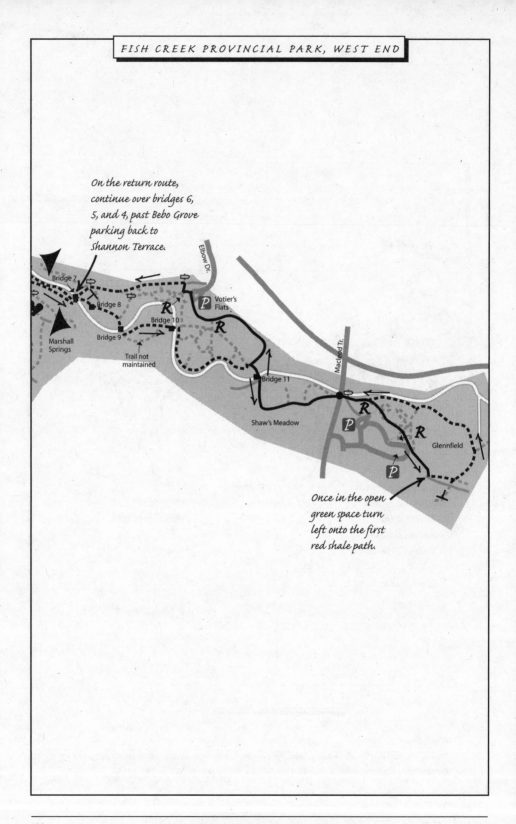

On the return route,
continue over bridges 6,
5, and 4, past Bebo Grove
parking back to
Shannon Terrace.

Elbow Dr.

Bridge 7

Bridge 8

Votier's
Flats

Marshall
Springs

Bridge 10

Bridge 9

Trail not
maintained

Macleod Tr.

Bridge 11

Shaw's Meadow

Glennfield

Once in the open
green space turn
left onto the first
red shale path.

FISH CREEK PROVINCIAL PARK/ MCKENZIE/DOUGLASDALE, SE

Categories: *paved pathway, nature, family, bike trailer–friendly, kids, rollerblade, non-stop, picnic, ice cream (summer), lunch (summer)*
Approximate Distance: *23 kilometres*
Terrain: *paved path, shale path, dirt road, quite street*
Degree of Difficulty: *easy with mostly flat terrain and one major hill climb*
Parking: *Fish Creek Provincial Park (Bow Valley Ranch): take Bow Bottom Trail SE into Fish Creek park; turn right into the Bow Valley Ranch parking lot; rollerblade parking: official Fish Creek parking lot at Mallard Point: follow Canyon Meadows Drive SE to the end.*
Rollerblade Route: *Cross the Bow River and follow the paved path up and along the escarpment. Enjoy wonderful mountain and Bow River views throughout the route.*
Facilities: *bathrooms, playgrounds, lake with lifeguards (summer), picnic tables, firepits*

Route at a Glance

Fish Creek Provincial Park is a great place to explore early in the morning, when you can hear and see more wildlife and avoid busy trails. At 8 AM on a warm May day, the songbirds, geese, mating grouse, and ducks are in full chorus, and the scent of flowering trees and shrubs is intoxicating. Pedal through mature forests on paved paths from Bow Valley Ranch to Sikome Lake. The ring road around the lake offers views of this popular summer swimming hole. A meandering shale path follows the Bow River and leads to a pedestrian bridge and the McKenzie Meadows Golf Course. Shrubs and poplar trees line the paved path along the course. A hill climb soon slows you down and gives you a better view of the manicured golf course and the wilds of Fish Creek Provincial Park beyond. Travel briefly through the community of Mountain Park to access the paved trail along the escarpment. Wow, what a view! The Rockies stretch along the western horizon, Fish Creek Provincial Park and the Bow River lie below, while the office towers of downtown Calgary sit on the northwest skyline. Listen for the croaking frogs that live in the McKenzie Meadows Golf Course wetlands and watch for pelicans on the Bow River. A gradual descent through the forest leads to a bridge crossing back into Fish Creek park. The pedalling is easy and smooth on the flat paved paths that lead back to Bow Valley Ranch.

Cautions/Highlights

This is a wonderful route for families. Since the starting point is in the middle of the circuit, the route can be shortened at the halfway point—a nice option for tired children and their parents.

BIRDS ON THE BOW RIVER

Watch for large American white pelicans fishing in the shallows in the Bow River from May through August. They're easy to spot from the escarpment trail above Fish Creek park. Pelicans usually nest on flat, treeless islands that keep them safe from predators. They frequent the Bow River from the Inglewood Bird Sanctuary all the way to Fish Creek Provincial Park and have now been seen as far west as Edworthy Park.

Pelicans are not the only birds calling Fish Creek home for part of the year. Spend some time around Mallard Point just after crossing the bridge at the far south end of this route to view the variety of birdlife in the park. The high canopy of balsam poplars makes for perfect nesting grounds. It's a noisy spot in the spring, when birds are fighting for prime locations with mountain views. Watch for big holes in old trees, where the cavity-nesters, such as woodpeckers, nuthatches, tree swallows, and wrens, hang their hats.

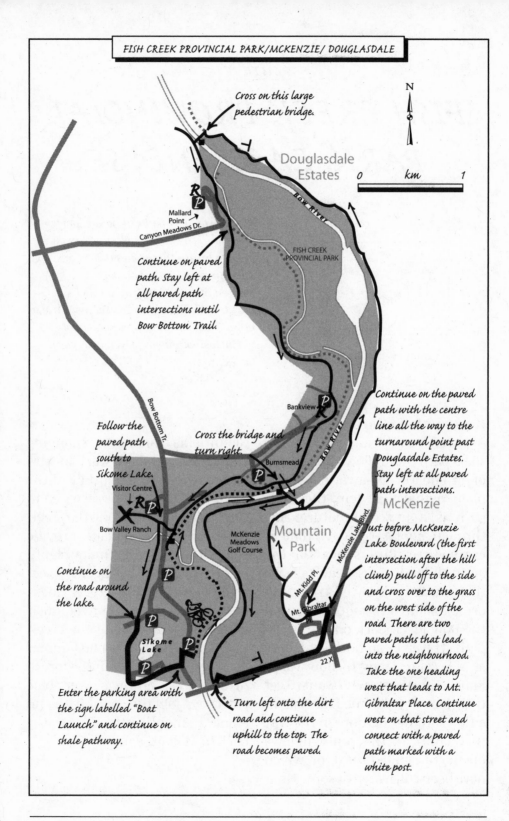

Cross on this large pedestrian bridge.

N

Douglasdale Estates

0   km   1

Bow River

Mallard Point

Canyon Meadows Dr.

FISH CREEK PROVINCIAL PARK

Continue on paved path. Stay left at all paved path intersections until Bow Bottom Trail.

Bow Bottom Tr.

Bankview

Bow River

Follow the paved path south to Sikome Lake.

Cross the bridge and turn right.

Burnsmead

Visitor Centre

Bow Valley Ranch

McKenzie Meadows Golf Course

Mountain Park

McKenzie Lake Blvd.

Continue on the paved path with the centre line all the way to the turnaround point past Douglasdale Estates. Stay left at all paved path intersections.

McKenzie

Just before McKenzie Lake Boulevard (the first intersection after the hill climb) pull off to the side and cross over to the grass on the west side of the road. There are two paved paths that lead into the neighbourhood. Take the one heading west that leads to Mt. Gibraltar Place. Continue west on that street and connect with a paved path marked with a white post.

Continue on the road around the lake.

Mt. Kidd Pl.

Mt. Gibraltar

Sikome Lake

22 X

Enter the parking area with the sign labelled "Boat Launch" and continue on shale pathway.

Turn left onto the dirt road and continue uphill to the top. The road becomes paved.

FISH CREEK PROVINCIAL PARK, EAST END, SE

Categories: *bike pathway, nature, family, bike trailer–friendly, kids, picnic, ice cream*
Approximate Distance: *19 kilometres*
Terrain: *paved path, shale path*
Degree of Difficulty: *easy and flat*
Parking: *Mallard Point: follow Canyon Meadows Drive SE east into the official parking lot*
Facilities: *bathrooms, playgrounds, picnic tables, firepits*

Route at a Glance

A paved path leads to the red shale path that follows a creek full of birdlife. Tucked away below the main pathway system, the shale path is a peaceful nature ride through poplar trees. Wildlife is everywhere! Bird songs fill the air in the mornings, beavers leave their mark on gnawed trees, and occasionally you'll spot pelicans on the Bow River. Back on the paved path, travel is smooth and easy as the route leads to Bow Valley Ranch. For cyclists who want to get their feet wet, Sikome Lake makes a fine summer detour. On the way to Glennfield, the route follows open grasslands, most of which have been cultivated at some time.

Glennfield's constantly changing wildflower displays start in May and continue until mid-July. At the Glennfield parking area, switch to the shale pathway along the creek, where balsam poplars provide shade for you and for many plants. In the spring, the pungent, sweet smell of wolf willow greets riders. In early mornings and at dusk, mule deer graze along the creek, and in the heat of a midsummer day, they take shelter in the forest. After a break on the slower shale pathways, join the paved path and enjoy a smooth ride all the way back to Mallard Point.

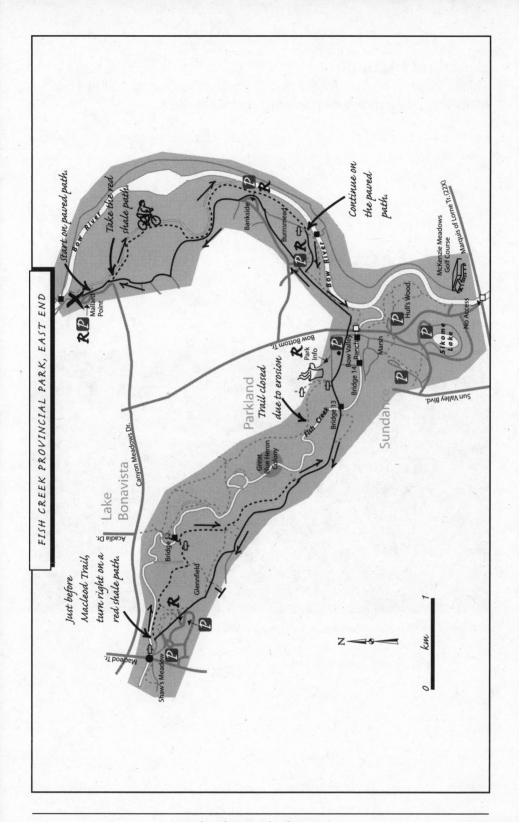

Start on paved path

Take the red shale path

Mallard Point

Bow River

Bankside

Burnsmead

Continue on the paved path.

Bow River

Hull's Wood

McKenzie Meadows Golf Course

Marquis of Lorne Tr. (22X)

No Access

Sikome Lake

Parkland

Trail closed due to erosion

Bow Bottom Tr.

Park Info

Bow Valley Ranch

Bridge 14

Marsh

Sundance

Sun Valley Blvd.

Lake Bonavista

Canyon Meadows Dr.

Acadia Dr.

Great Blue Heron Colony

Fish Creek

Bridge 13

Bridge 12

Glenfield

Just before Macleod Trail, turn right on a red shale path

Macleod Tr.

Shaw's Meadow

N

0   km   1

Cautions/Highlights

This is the perfect route for families of all ages and a nice spring warm- up route for adults pulling children in bike trailers.

Wide open grasslands near Bow Valley Ranch host wildflowers and wildlife.

Calgary's Best Long Bike Rides

(approximate route start location and loop length)

ROUTES BY NUMBER

- **27** North Calgary (50 km)
- **28** Peak to Peak (Nose Hill Park/ Broadcast Hill) (45 km)
- **29** River Valley Ride (50 km)
- **30** Glenmore Reservoir/Elbow River (43 km)
- **31** Irrigation Canal to Chestermere (53 km)
- **32** South Calgary (55 km)
- **33** Tour de Calgary Figure Eight (110 km)

NORTH CALGARY, NW/NE

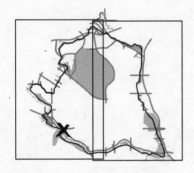

Categories: *paved pathway, family, bike trailer–friendly, kids, non-stop, picnic, ice cream, lunch, coffee shop*
Approximate Distance: *50 kilometres*
Terrain: *paved path, quiet streets*
Degree of Difficulty: *difficult with lots of hills*
Parking: *far south parking on north side of Edworthy Park: At the intersection of Bowness Road and Shaganappi Trail NW, turn onto Montgomery View and continue to the parking areas; far north parking at West Nose Creek Park: official parking lot at the corner of Beddington Trail and Beddington Boulevard NE*
Facilities: *bathrooms (Edworthy Park and West Nose Creek Park), playgrounds, picnic tables, water park at Eau Claire*
Ice Cream: *Confetti Ice Cream: 4416–5 Street NE (Nose Creek Pathway)*

Route at a Glance

The pathway system in Calgary's north is the quietest in the city. It's perfect for serious cyclists who want to go hard and steady, but it also offers a few good reasons to stop when you need a break. Start along familiar terrain on the Bow River Pathway and cycle into Bowmont Natural Environment Park, one of Calgary's little-known gems. Continue uphill to mountain and river views before travelling a few streets through Varsity. Back on the paved path, the route travels through a green space tucked away in Dalhousie before winding along the streets of Edgemont. Back onto the paved path, you soon enter Edgemont Park Ravines, a manicured ravine park with playgrounds, landscaped ponds, and picnic tables. Next along the route is a wilderness ravine, where coyotes cross the path without much warning and mule deer munch and rest in the shrubbery.

Travel along paved paths through the Hidden Valley neighbourhood in the far north. Riders with a passion for hills and views can take the optional hill to the top of the sandstone outcrops in Panorama Hills. Onward to West Nose Creek Park with its mix of bridges, dirt trails, and the paved path. The Nose Creek Pathway, which follows the train tracks, is usually very quiet. Pedalling this part of the route is fast and steady, unless you stop for ice cream at Confetti's (4416–5 Street NE). Back on the Bow River Pathway you'll start to see more people. The trail is flat all the way back to Edworthy Park.

Cautions/Highlights

This very hilly route is perfect for riders who want a half-day, non-stop ride.

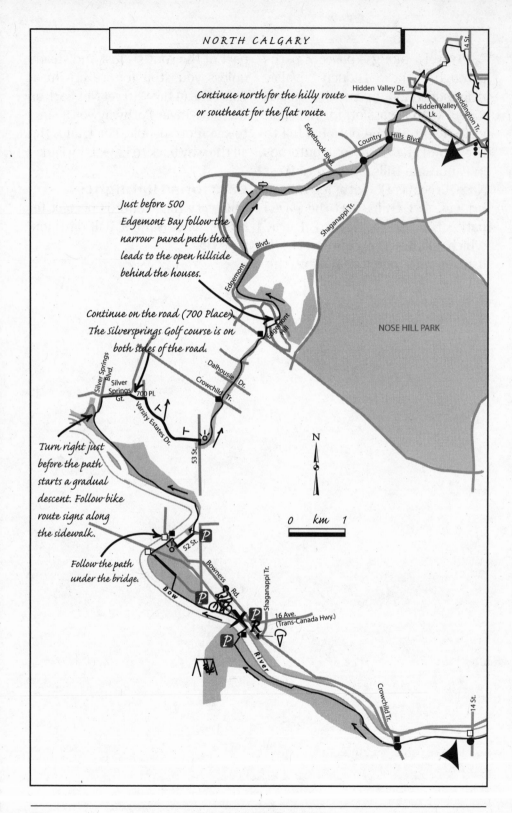

Continue north for the hilly route or southeast for the flat route.

Hidden Valley Dr.

Hidden Valley Lk.

Edgebrook Blvd

Country Hills Blvd

Beddington Tr.

14 St.

Just before 500 Edgemont Bay follow the narrow paved path that leads to the open hillside behind the houses.

Shaganappi Tr.

Edgemont ___ Blvd.

NOSE HILL PARK

Continue on the road (700 Place). The Silversprings Golf course is on both sides of the road.

Edgemont Hill

Dalhousie Dr.

Silver Springs Blvd.

Silver Springs Gt.

700 Pl.

Crowchild Tr.

Varsity Estates Dr.

53 St.

N

Turn right just before the path starts a gradual descent. Follow bike route signs along the sidewalk.

0   km   1

52 St.

Follow the path under the bridge.

Bow

Bowness Rd.

Shaganappi Tr.

16 Ave. (Trans-Canada Hwy.)

River

Crowchild Tr.

14 St.

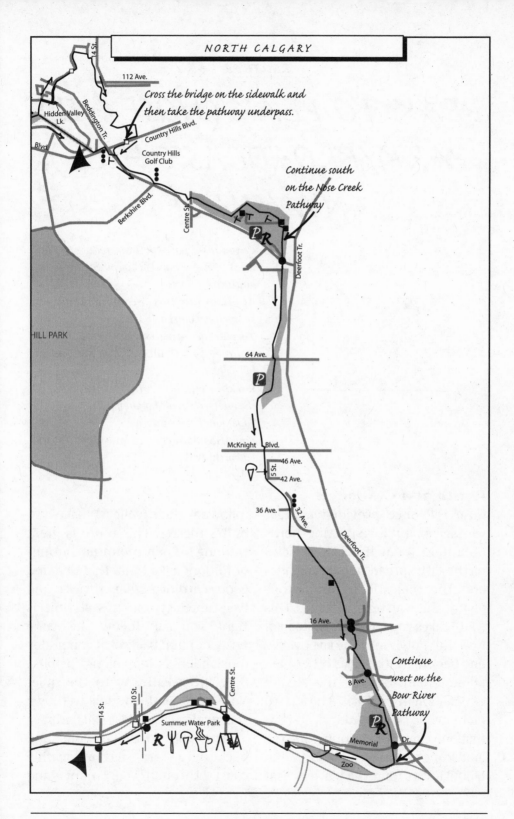

Cross the bridge on the sidewalk and then take the pathway underpass.

Continue south on the Nose Creek Pathway

Continue west on the Bow River Pathway

14 St.

112 Ave.

Hidden Valley Lk.

Beddington Tr.

Blvd.

Country Hills Blvd.

Country Hills Golf Club

Berkshire Blvd.

Centre St.

HILL PARK

Deerfoot Tr.

64 Ave.

McKnight Blvd.

46 Ave.

5 St.

42 Ave.

36 Ave.

32 Ave.

Deerfoot Tr.

16 Ave.

8 Ave.

Memorial Dr.

Zoo

14 St.

10 St.

Centre St.

Summer Water Park

PEAK TO PEAK (NOSE HILL PARK/BROADCAST HILL), NW/SW/SE

Categories: *paved pathway, nature, family, bike trailer–friendly, kids, picnic, ice cream, lunch, coffee shop*
Approximate Distance: *Out and Back: 30 kilometres; Long Loop: 45 kilometres*
Terrain: *paved path, quiet street*
Degree of Difficulty: *difficult with lots of hill climbing*
Parking: *official Nose Hill Park parking at the intersection of Shaganappi Trail and Edgemont Boulevard NW*
Facilities: *bathrooms at Nose Hill Park and Edworthy Park*

Route at a Glance

Nose Hill once provided a great vantage point for spotting herds of buffalo. Today it provides views of the city spread out on all sides and the majestic mountaintops along the western skyline. This route takes you from the plateau of Nose Hill, down into the river valley, and back up to the city's other high point, Broadcast Hill, the site of Canada Olympic Park. These two plateaus are remnants of a sixty-million-year-old swampy, forested landscape into which the Bow and Elbow Rivers (and the glaciers that followed their valleys) have cut by 175 metres. This route is great training for hilly mountain outings or for long bike tours that demand good cardiovascular fitness and well-tuned cycling legs. If time is tight, you can follow the same route out and back, or, if you prefer, make a longer loop along the busy Bow River Pathway to the quiet Nose Creek Pathway, followed by a short ride across Nose Hill Park.

Out and Back: The out and back route starts with a downhill coast through Edgemont and the green space in Dalhousie. A short stint on the streets of Varsity leads to Bowmont Natural Environment Park, where the Bow River Pathway makes pedalling a pleasure. Continue on the flat, paved path through Shouldice Park to Edworthy Park, where the climbing begins. Follow Edworthy Street up, up, and away to the quiet streets of Patterson Heights. This neighbourhood is full of brand new homes, with the exception of one old farm with grazing horses that sits in the middle of the suburban sprawl. The final climb on a hillside paved path leads to wonderful views. To return to your car, turn and follow your tracks back to Nose Hill Park.

The Loop: Head east across Nose Hill Park on wide dirt paths, then follow the paved path that goes under 14 Street NW. Soon you are on the quiet Nose Creek Pathway, where you can pick up the pace and pedal hard. Enjoy the cardiovascular challenge while you can because the Bow River Pathway, often crowded with people, is next en route. Cross over St. Patrick's Island to the south side of the river and enjoy flat, easy biking all the way to Edworthy Park. The slow slog up Edworthy Street is a necessary evil to access the panoramic views of Broadcast Hill. The climb is followed by a breezy glide back to the river valley, after which you head west to Bowmont Natural Environment Park. A gradual climb leads to the streets of Varsity and a paved-path ride through backdoor green spaces in Dalhousie and Edgemont. The last climb out of Edgemont leads you back to your car at Nose Hill Park.

Cautions/Highlights

This route provides a great workout without crowds of people.

Soak up the big-sky view from the Nose Hill Park plateau.

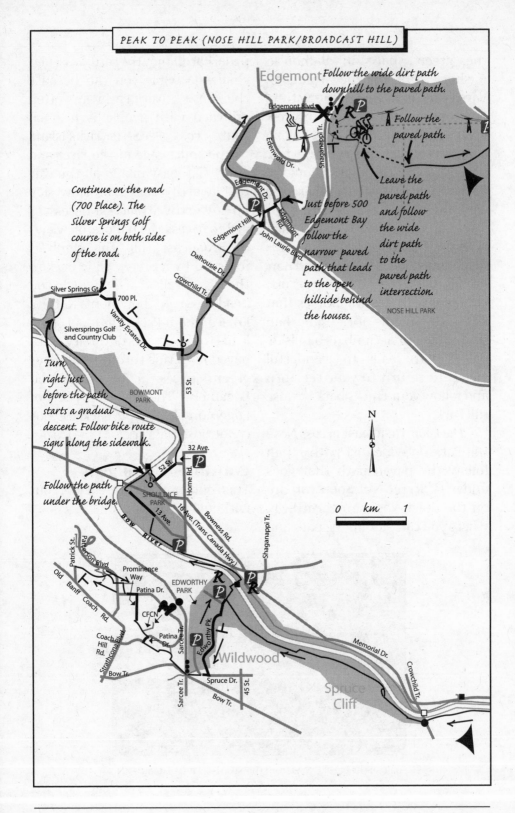

Edgemont

Follow the wide dirt path downhill to the paved path.

Follow the paved path.

Leave the paved path and follow the wide dirt path to the paved path intersection.

Continue on the road (700 Place). The Silver Springs Golf course is on both sides of the road.

Just before 500 Edgemont Bay follow the narrow paved path that leads to the open hillside behind the houses.

NOSE HILL PARK

Silver Springs Gt.

700 Pl.

Silversprings Golf and Country Club

Turn right just before the path starts a gradual descent. Follow bike route signs along the sidewalk.

BOWMONT PARK

Follow the path under the bridge.

SHOULDICE PARK

N

0   km   1

EDWORTHY PARK

Wildwood

Spruce Cliff

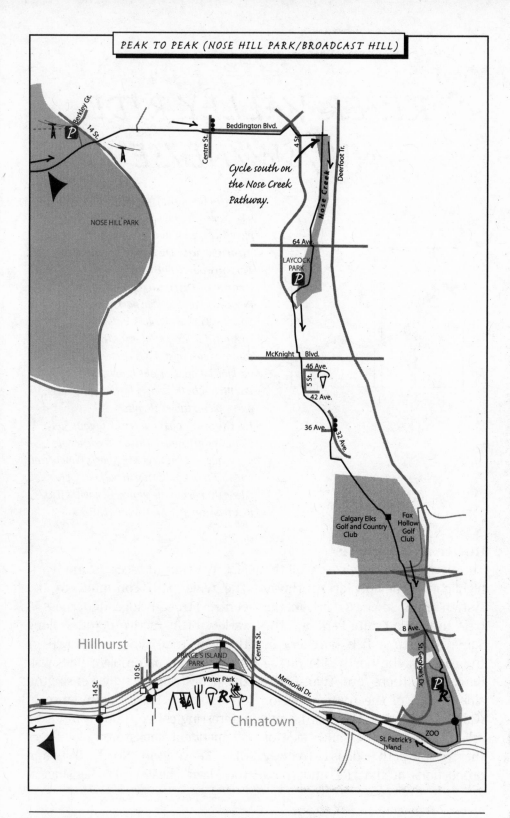

Cycle south on
the Nose Creek
Pathway.

RIVER VALLEY RIDE, NW/SW/NE/SE

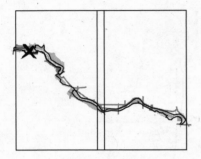

Categories: *paved pathway, nature, family, bike trailer–friendly, kids, rollerblade, non-stop, picnic, ice cream, lunch, coffee shop*
Approximate Distance: *50 kilometres*
Terrain: *paved path, quiet street*
Degree of Difficulty: *moderate*
Parking: *West: official parking lots at Bowness Park, 8900–48 Avenue NW; East: official parking lot on St. George's Drive NE; continue east past the zoo, down the hill to the parking lot on the right-hand side*
Facilities: *bathrooms, playgrounds, water parks, picnic tables, firepits*
Ice Cream: *Moo's Country Ice Cream, Eau Claire Market; Angel's Drive Inn, corner of 47 Avenue and 85 Street NW; Angel's Cappuccino and Ice Cream, at the north parking lot for Edworthy Park in the summer; Leavitt's (Lics) Ice Cream Shop, 3410–3 Avenue NW*

Route at a Glance

This paved-path route covers all the highlights of the Bow River Pathway system from Bowness Park in the west to Pearce Estate Park and the Sam Livingstone fish hatchery in the east. On the north side of the Bow River, there are two paths along much of the route—one for walkers, the other for cyclists and rollerbladers. On the south side of the river, the path widens to freeway proportions at the LRT underpass just west of Prince's Island Park. The wide path continues to the Centre Street Bridge underpass. A variety of attractive detours along the way may slow you down or bring you to a complete halt. Visit the pedestrian-friendly Kensington area, known for its abundance of interesting coffee shops, a fantastic independent bookstore called Pages (1135 Kensington Road NW), and the Plaza Theatre (1133 Kensington

Road NW), where you can see all the world films that don't make it to mainstream theatres. The zoo is a fun stop during the day year-round. From June through September, the zoo's annual and perennial flower gardens are spectacular, and if you are ever in need of some rain forest moisture, check out the butterfly house or the gorillas' new home in Destination Africa.

On the return route, stop at Eau Claire Market for an ice cream or coffee on the square, or at the Eau Claire YMCA for an economy priced bacon and eggs breakfast. For a more cultured outing, stop for an evening outdoor theatre performance on Prince's Island Park, where Shakespeare in the Park plays during summer months. This is a vibrant route in the heart of Calgary that offers riders the choice of smooth, non-stop pedalling or a mix of stops and starts that lasts the entire day.

Cautions/Highlights

The Bow River Pathway is extremely busy in the summer, especially near Prince's Island Park, where festivals take place July 1 and every weekend from June through August.

POPLAR TRAITS

When you hit the trails in June, get ready for some fuzzy poplar fluff along the Bow River Pathway. Poplar trees are dioecious, which means the species has both male and female trees. If pollination occurs, the females produce vast numbers of parachuting seeds that take flight in June. The seeds find their way up your nose, or worse, into your mouth, as you coast along the pathway. If, however, Calgary has had a late-spring frost or extreme winter weather, poplar seeds may be almost non-existent in the spring.

The fluff is not the only distinctive poplar trait. When cycling in the spring, you may notice the distinctive aroma that a balsam poplar emits. The scent comes from their resin, which the Cree once used to stop bleeding.

ANGEL'S CAPPUCCINO AND ICE CREAM CAFÉ

Stop in at Angel's Café to fuel up or cool down. Whether you'd like a full meal, a muffin and coffee, or an ice cream and cold drink, Angel's is perfectly situated to quench hunger and thirst. Location: Edworthy Park North: along the Bow River Pathway near the parking lot on the north side of Edworthy Park.

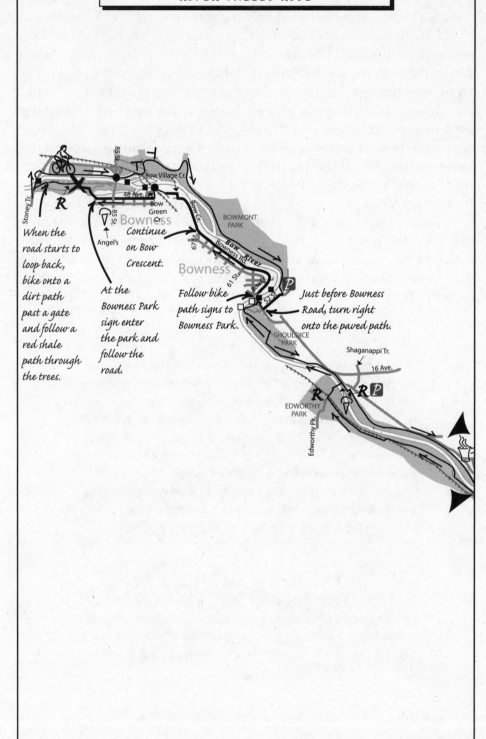

When the road starts to loop back, bike onto a dirt path past a gate and follow a red shale path through the trees.

At the Bowness Park sign enter the park and follow the road.

Continue on Bow Crescent.

Follow bike path signs to Bowness Park.

Just before Bowness Road, turn right onto the paved path.

Stoney Tr.

85 St.

Bow Village Cr.

48 Ave.

Bow Green Crs.

Angel's

85 St.

Bowness

Bow Cr.

69 St.

BOWMONT PARK

Bowness

Bow River

Bowness Rd.

61 St.

52 St.

SHOULDICE PARK

Shaganappi Tr.

16 Ave.

EDWORTHY PARK

Edworthy Pk.

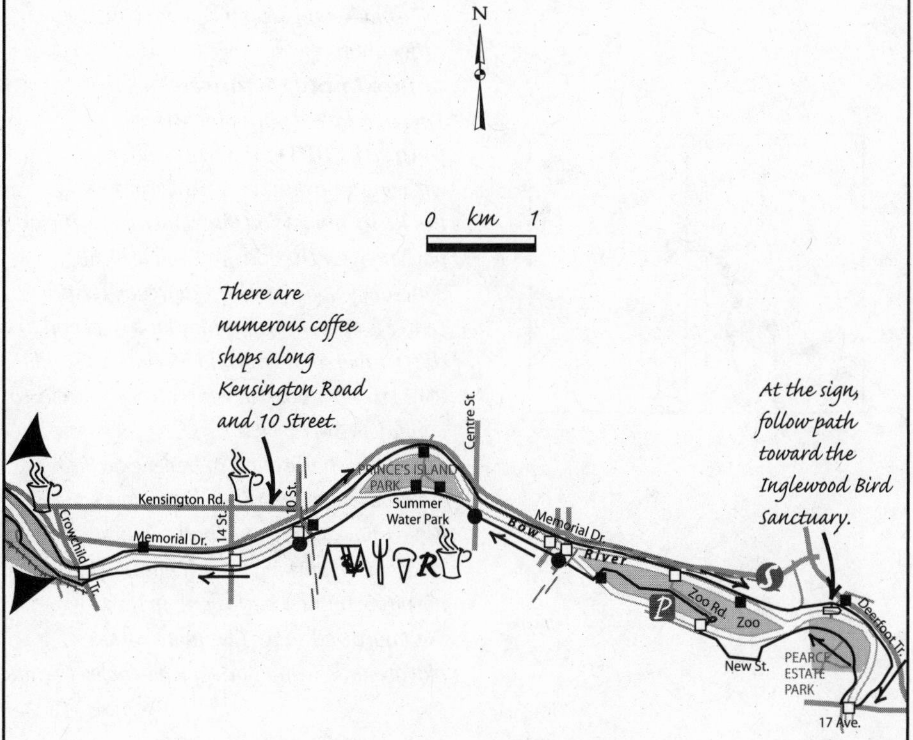

N

0 km 1

There are numerous coffee shops along Kensington Road and 10 Street.

At the sign, follow path toward the Inglewood Bird Sanctuary.

Kensington Rd.

Centre St.

Crowchild Tr.

Memorial Dr.

14 St.

10 St.

PRINCE'S ISLAND PARK

Summer Water Park

Bow River

Memorial Dr

P

Zoo Rd.

Zoo

New St.

Deerfoot Tr.

PEARCE ESTATE PARK

17 Ave.

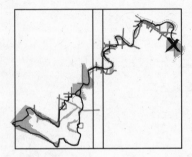

GLENMORE RESERVOIR/ ELBOW RIVER, SW

Categories: *paved pathway, neighbourhood, nature, family, bike trailer–friendly, kids, rollerblade, non-stop, picnic, ice cream, lunch, coffee shop*
Approximate Distance: *43 kilometres*
Terrain: *paved path, quiet street*
Degree of Difficulty: *easy and mostly flat with one long descent and hill climb*
Parking: *Inglewood Bird Sanctuary, official parking near the end of 9 Avenue SE at Sanctuary Road. The bird sanctuary visitor centre is open from the May long weekend to the October long weekend, Monday to Sunday, 10 AM to 5 PM; open in winter from Tuesday to Sunday, 10 AM to 4 PM*
Facilities: *bathrooms at Inglewood Bird Sanctuary during visitor centre hours listed above; year-round bathrooms at the Weaselhead parking lot, just past Rockyview hospital; summer bathrooms in North Glenmore and South Glenmore Parks; playgrounds, water parks, picnic tables, firepits*

Route at a Glance

This route offers the perfect combination of nature, homes, and gardens. Start at the Inglewood Bird Sanctuary, a 32-hectare wildlife reserve, where you can see more than 270 different species of birds at various times throughout the year. In the spring, songbirds populate the large trees along the Elbow River Pathway, making for a musical early-morning ride. Watch for interesting architecture and inspiring gardens during the short jaunts through Mission and

Riverdale. Continue past Sandy Beach and watch for dogs, kids, canoeists, kayakers, and rafters all enjoying the water on a hot summer day. A hill climb takes you closer to Weaselhead Flats Natural Area, where you're likely to spot bald eagles, hawks, all kinds of ducks, geese, and goslings (in the spring), and red-winged blackbirds. Keen birders, using binoculars, will be busy keeping watch for the more than two hundred bird species that frequent the park, including ruby-throated hummingbirds and tundra swans, which visit every spring until their northern nesting grounds thaw out.

The pathway descends into the Weaselhead, where the trees are large and you feel immersed in the wilderness. Pedal past wetlands and up a long hill to the poplar-lined pathway on the south side of the reservoir. A wonderful, smooth stretch of pathway leads past the sailing club toward Glenmore Landing, a nice shopping area to make a pit stop for coffee or lunch. Watch for large groups of inland gulls floating on the reservoir in the spring and Canada geese at dusk in the fall. Every evening around sunset in late fall, hundreds of geese test their migratory v-shaped flying skills as they land in flocks on the reservoir. Cycle over the dam back to the Elbow River Pathway and your car.

Cautions/Highlights
The reservoir route is busy on weekends throughout the spring, summer, and fall, but part of the route has separate paths for walkers and cyclists.

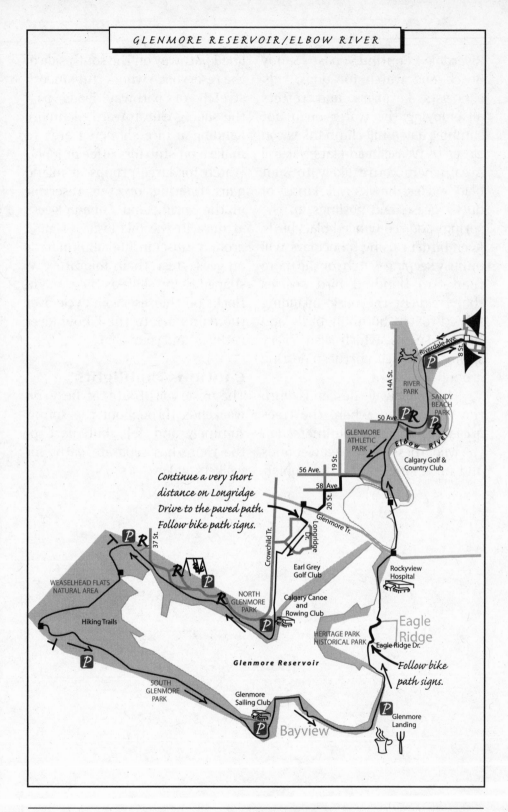

Continue a very short distance on Longridge Drive to the paved path. Follow bike path signs.

Riverdale Ave.

8 St.

14A St.

RIVER PARK

SANDY BEACH PARK

50 Ave.

GLENMORE ATHLETIC PARK

Elbow River

Calgary Golf & Country Club

56 Ave.

19 St.

58 Ave.

20 St.

Crowchild Tr.

Glenmore Tr.

Longridge Dr.

37 St.

WEASELHEAD FLATS NATURAL AREA

Hiking Trails

NORTH GLENMORE PARK

Earl Grey Golf Club

Calgary Canoe and Rowing Club

Rockyview Hospital

Eagle Ridge

HERITAGE PARK HISTORICAL PARK

Eagle Ridge Dr.

Follow bike path signs.

SOUTH GLENMORE PARK

Glenmore Reservoir

Glenmore Sailing Club

Bayview

Glenmore Landing

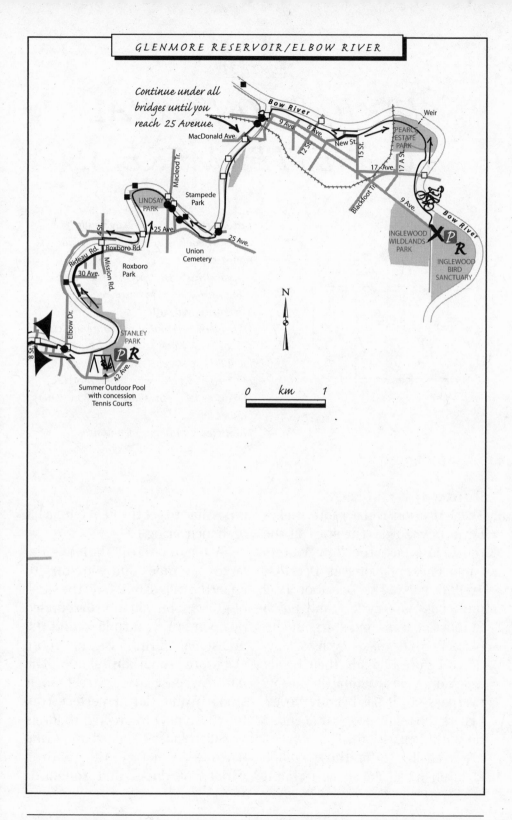

Continue under all bridges until you reach 25 Avenue.

Bow River

9 Ave.

8 Ave.

New St.

MacDonald Ave.

Macleod Tr.

12 St.

15 St.

Weir

PEARCE ESTATE PARK

17 Ave.

17 A St.

LINDSAY PARK

Stampede Park

Blackfoot Tr.

9 Ave.

Bow River

1 St.

25 Ave.

25 Ave.

Union Cemetery

INGLEWOOD WILDLANDS PARK

INGLEWOOD BIRD SANCTUARY

Bideau Rd.

Roxboro Rd.

Mission Rd.

30 Ave.

Roxboro Park

N

Elbow Dr.

STANLEY PARK

8 St.

42 Ave.

Summer Outdoor Pool
with concession
Tennis Courts

0   km   1

IRRIGATION CANAL TO CHESTERMERE, SE

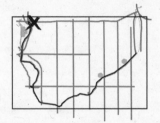

Categories: *paved pathway, family, bike trailer–friendly (sort of), kids, rollerblade, non-stop, picnic*
Approximate Distance: *53 kilometres round trip to Lake Chestermere*
Terrain: *paved path*
Degree of Difficulty: *moderate/difficult*
Parking: *Bow Waters Canoe Club parking lot at 1975–26 Street SE; the club is just east of Deerfoot, off 17 Avenue SE and 26 Street SE/Barlow; follow the signs to the Bow Waters Canoe Club*
Facilities: *bathrooms, picnic tables*

Route at a Glance

The irrigation canal route makes for a unique ride. The start of the route, just past the Bow Waters Canoe Club and alongside Deerfoot Trail, is noisy. The Deerfoot Trail underpass is very low and has a number of stops and starts due to barriers that make cyclists slow down before bonking their heads. There once was padding on the low overpass, but it has been removed. I guess too many people still ended up with concussions. The barriers are a challenge for those pulling children in wide bike trailers, but it is possible to get through with a bit of maneuvering.

At Glenmore Trail, the industrial landscape fades and you start to enjoy the calls of birds and the smell of grass. Soon you are surrounded by open prairie farmland and the occasional farmhouse or more elaborate suburban abode. The pathway east of 52 Street SE is smooth and flat, a perfect trail for those new to cycling, children, or rollerbladers. The urban outing becomes a nature ride with a variety of ducks and songbirds floating and flying along the canal at various times throughout the year. Pass managed wetlands and the Heather Glen Golf Course before reaching Chestermere Lake. This man-made lake, fed by the Bow River, is 5.6 kilometres long and 0.8 kilometres wide. Cycle along West Chestermere Drive, around the lake to East Chestermere Drive, where restaurants and convenience stores offer drinks and snacks. Alternatively, you can travel Chestermere Drive, East and West, around the lake to a restaurant, or settle down for a picnic lunch on the shore. This route is open to the elements, with no shade relief east of Glenmore Trail. If chinook winds are blowing, the ride back will be a slow slog.

Cautions/Highlights

If chinook winds are blowing, the ride back into Calgary can be very hard work.

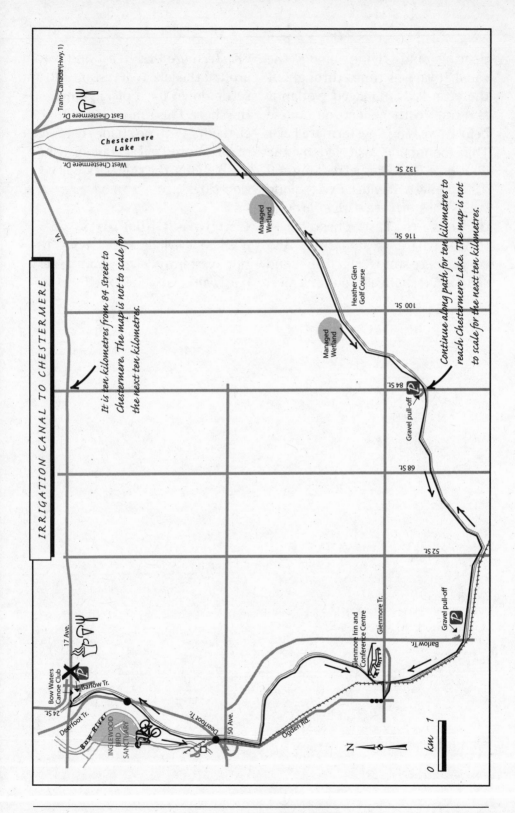

IRRIGATION CANAL TO CHESTERMERE

It is ten kilometres from 84 Street to Chestermere. The map is not to scale for the next ten kilometres.

Continue along path for ten kilometres to reach Chestermere Lake. The map is not to scale for the next ten kilometres.

Chestermere Lake

Trans-Canada (Hwy. 1)

East Chestermere Dr.

West Chestermere Dr.

1A

Managed Wetland

Managed Wetland

Heather Glen Golf Course

132 St.

116 St.

100 St.

84 St.

68 St.

52 St.

Gravel pull-off

Bow Waters Canoe Club

17 Ave.

Barlow Tr.

24 St.

Deerfoot Tr.

Bow River

INGLEWOOD BIRD SANCTUARY

Deerfoot Tr.

50 Ave.

Ogden Rd.

Glenmore Inn and Conference Centre

Glenmore Tr.

Barlow Tr.

Gravel pull-off

N

0   km   1

SOUTH CALGARY, SW/SE

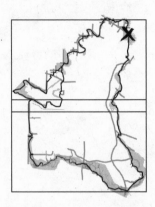

Categories: *paved pathway, nature, family, bike trailer–friendly, kids, non-stop, picnic, lunch, coffee shop*
Approximate Distance: *55 kilometres*
Terrain: *paved path, shale path*
Degree of Difficulty: *difficult with many hills*
Parking: *Inglewood Bird Sanctuary: official parking lot near the end of 9 Avenue SE at Sanctuary Road; Alternate Parking: official Weaselhead parking off 37 Street SW in North Glenmore Park*
Facilities: *bathrooms at parks along the route, playgrounds, picnic tables, firepits*

Route at a Glance

The smooth, flat start to this route provides the perfect warm-up for the next four or five hours of biking. It's pleasant pedalling to Fish Creek Provincial Park along the 37 Street green space. Choose your route through the park and, on a hot day, enjoy the shady relief of full-grown trees in the park's west end. The route travels over bridges, along Fish Creek, and once east of Macleod Trail, opens into summer wildflower-filled meadows. Watch for mule deer throughout the park, and as the path comes close to the Bow River near the Bankview parking area, keep a sharp lookout for groups of pelicans fishing in the shallows. Back on the Bow River Pathway, continue past Carburn Park and Beaver Dam Flats Park. The trail can be noisy with traffic, trains, and industry on the eastern portion of the route. It's good to know that someone is keeping the economy alive while you're out enjoying a self-propelled adventure! Pass the Inglewood Bird Sanctuary and enjoy a short stint on the streets of Inglewood before turning south onto the Elbow River Pathway. This is the "culture" part of the outing, especially during the second week of July, when the

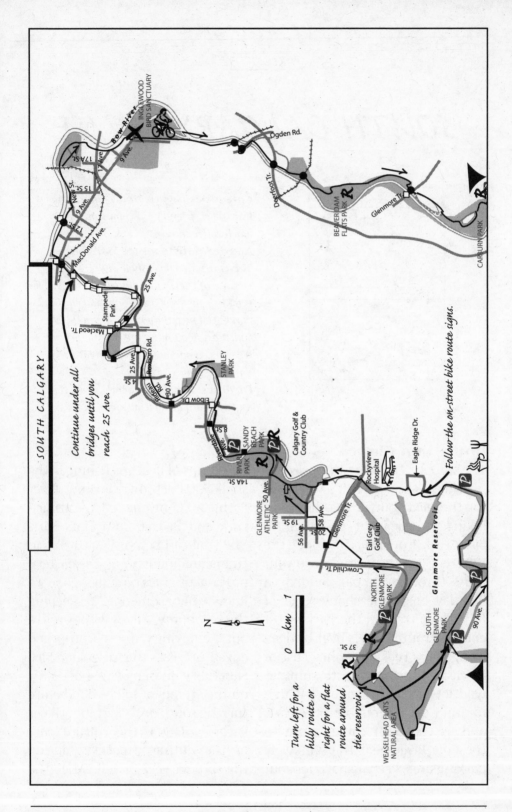

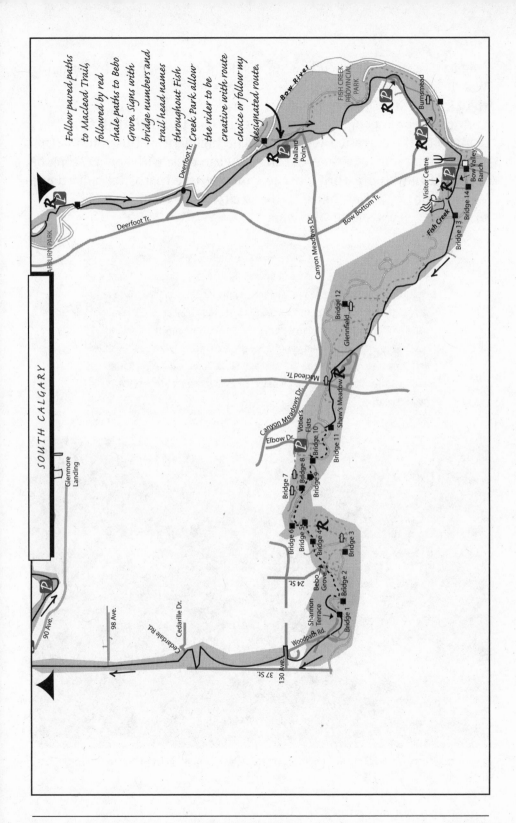

Follow paved paths to Macleod Trail, followed by red shale paths to Bebo Grove. Signs with bridge numbers and trail head names throughout Fish Creek Park allow the rider to be creative with route choice or follow my designated route.

SOUTH CALGARY

Calgary Stampede is in full swing. Watch for people rafting along the Elbow River. On very hot days in August, some people just swim along with the current. Cycle back to the reservoir, where you can choose a hilly route through the Weaselhead or a flat route with mountain views along the east side of the reservoir to return to your car.

Cautions/Highlights

The highlight of this route is that you can cycle with so few stops, on mostly paved paths, for half a day in a city of one million people.

WOLF WILLOW

When you travel along Calgary pathways in June, the pungent smell of the wolf willow in flower is your constant companion. This smell is unique to the Prairies, and it means that summer is just around the corner. The official name of this plant is silverberry, but wolf willow is the name more commonly used, even though the plant is not a willow. Wolf willow is an upright shrub with silver leaves. Its yellow flowers appear in June and July, followed by silver berries. The flowers can be detected from many metres away by their heavy scent.

A footbridge across the Elbow River allows cyclists to pedal non-stop from one community to the next.

TOUR DE CALGARY FIGURE EIGHT, NE/NW/SE/SW

Categories: *paved pathway, nature, culture, family, bike trailer–friendly, kids, non-stop, hill training, picnic, ice cream, lunch, coffee shop*
Approximate Distance: *110 kilometres*
Terrain: *paved path, quiet streets*
Degree of Difficulty: *difficult*
Parking: *Just past the north parking lots for the zoo is an official parking lot on St. George's Drive NE for the Nose Creek Pathway; continue east past the zoo, down the hill to the parking lot on the right-hand side*
Facilities: *bathrooms, playgrounds, water parks, picnic tables, firepits*

Route at a Glance

Who would have thought that you could bike a full day in Calgary on mostly paved paths with almost no stops and very few major intersections? Calgary has more than 400 kilometres of paved pathways connecting the Bow and Elbow Rivers, Fish Creek Provincial Park, Nose Creek and West Nose Creek Parks, the Western Irrigation District Canal, and the perimeter of Glenmore Reservoir. This route takes you along all of these pathways except for the one along the Western Irrigation District Canal.

Start near the zoo on the Nose Creek Pathway. It's smooth sailing along this quiet pathway all the way to West Nose Creek Park. Choose between hilly or flat terrain along the north end of the city before descending into Edgemont Park Ravines. Watch for coyotes and deer crossing the paths and enjoy the various bird calls from the Edgemont wetland. Pedestrian overpasses keep you out of major traffic, and a short stint of on-street biking leads through the Varsity Estates neighbourhood into Bowmont Natural Environment Park. Travel along the Bow River

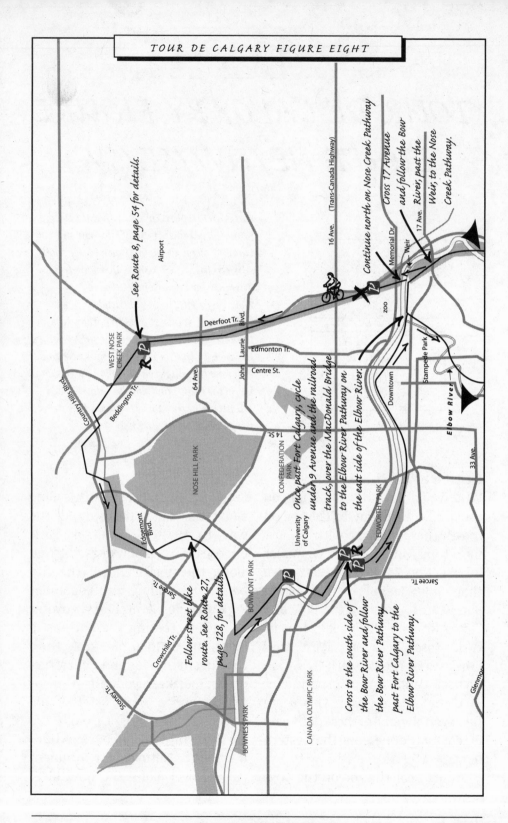

TOUR DE CALGARY FIGURE EIGHT

See Route 8, page 54 for details.

Continue north on Nose Creek Pathway

Cross 17 Avenue and follow the Bow River, past the Weir, to the Nose Creek Pathway.

(Trans-Canada Highway)

16 Ave.

Memorial Dr.

Weir

17 Ave.

zoo

Airport

Deerfoot Tr. Blvd.

WEST NOSE CREEK PARK

Laurie Blvd.

Edmonton Tr.

John

Centre St.

64 Ave.

Beddington Tr.

Country Hills Blvd.

14 St.

CONFEDERATION PARK

Stampede Park

Downtown

Elbow River

33 Ave.

Once past Fort Calgary, cycle under 9 Avenue and the railroad track, over the MacDonald Bridge to the Elbow River Pathway on the east side of the Elbow River.

NOSE HILL PARK

University of Calgary

Edgemont Blvd.

Sarcee Tr.

Crowchild Tr.

Follow street bike route. See Route 27, page 128, for details.

BOWMONT PARK

EDWORTH PARK

Sarcee Tr.

Glenmore

BOWNESS PARK

Stoney Tr.

CANADA OLYMPIC PARK

Cross to the south side of the Bow River and follow the Bow River Pathway past Fort Calgary to the Elbow River Pathway.

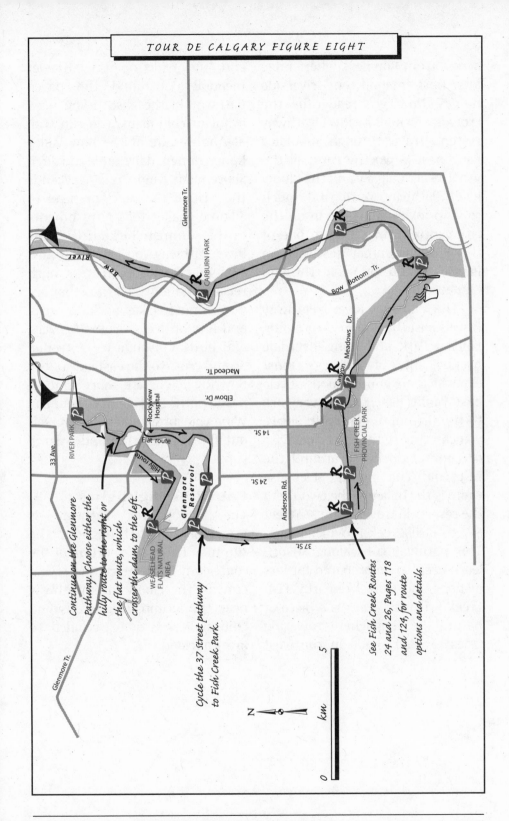

Continue on the Glenmore Pathway. Choose either the hilly route to the right or the flat route, which crosses the dam, to the left.

Cycle the 37 Street pathway to Fish Creek Park.

See Fish Creek Routes 24 and 26, Pages 118 and 124, for route options and details.

N

0 km 5

across from Bowness, where huge lots host magnificent riverside homes. Now get ready for the crowds on the Bow River Pathway system! Travel through Shouldice Park, past Edworthy Park, all the way to Fort Calgary and the Elbow River Pathway. You'll find much to stop for as you close in on the city centre. Plan a trip to one of the many summer festivals on Prince's Island, or pedal through Chinatown.

The Elbow River Pathway travels past the Stampede grounds, Lindsay Park, and along Riverdale Avenue, one of Calgary's most expensive neighbourhoods. Cycle past Sandy Beach and River Park to the Glenmore Reservoir, where you can choose to travel clockwise or counter-clockwise around the reservoir. The counter-clockwise route is the hillier of the two. From the reservoir, travel along 37 Street SW to Fish Creek Provincial Park. This pathway runs along an off-leash area, so be prepared for lots of dogs and walkers nearby. Fish Creek Provincial Park is a piece of natural heaven, where towering trees provide shade in the west end and wide open wildflower meadows surround the paved pathway in the east. If you need a hot or cold drink, you can stop at Annie's Café at the Bow Valley Ranch (open daily June through September and on weekends the rest of the year), or head to Sikome Lake for refreshments in the summer. Back on the Bow River Pathway, you'll pass Carburn Park and Beaver Dam Flats, both reclaimed industrial sites that are now home to lakes, walking paths, and lots of deer, coyotes, beavers, and birds. Continue to 17 Avenue SE and cross to the east side of the Bow River, where a short stint on paved paths leads back to your car. Wipe your brow and take yourself out for a cold drink and a large supper!

Cautions/Highlights

The Bow River Pathway is extremely busy throughout the summer. Travel this portion of the route early in the morning to avoid crowds. The Elbow River Pathway near the Stampede grounds and Lindsay Park is quite secluded, so bring a friend.

APPENDIX

The Best of Calgary's
Best Bike Rides and Trails

This appendix has categorized the bike routes to suit a variety of interests. *Foodie rides* lead you past tasty coffee shops, delis or ice cream vendors. *Family rides* follow bike paths or quiet side streets, have playground stops en route and an ice cream stop close-by. For those who like to get on the bike and go for it, try the *non-stop* rides that follow the paved paths and have very few stops. Get off the beaten path and explore Calgary's communities on the *neighbourhood home-and-garden rides*. Park your bike and explore Calgary's funky shopping and café districts on the *urban adventure rides*. Read through the categories below to help you choose your next urban cycling adventure.

Family Rides (follows bike paths or quiet side streets; perfect for bike trailers)
    Route 1: Baker Park/Bowness Park, NW
    Route 2 : Edgemont Park Ravines, NW
    Route 3: Airport, NE
    Route 4: Confederation Park, NW
    Route 6: Griffith Woods, SW
    Route 7: Bowmont Park/Scenic Acres Ravines, NW
    Route 8: West Nose Creek Park/Nose Hill Park, NW
    Route 9: Nose Hill Park (Flat), NW
    Route 10: Nose Hill Park (Hilly), NW
    Route 11: Bowness/Bowmont Park, NW
    Route 13: Nose Creek/West Nose Creek Park, NE
    Route 17: Inglewood/Mount Royal/Scotsman's Hill, SE/SW
    Route 18: Inglewood Bird Sanctuary/Carburn Park, SE
    Route 19: Garrison Woods/Mount Royal/Glenmore Reservoir, SW
    Route 20: Mount Royal/River Valley/Knob Hill, SW
    Route 21: Glenmore Reservoir/Fish Creek Provincial Park, SW
    Route 22: Glenmore Reservoir, SW
    Route 23: Carburn Park/Douglasdale/Fish Creek Provincial Park, SE
    Route 24: Fish Creek Provincial Park, West End, SW
    Route 25: Fish Creek Provincial Park/McKenzie/Douglasdale, SE
    Route 26: Fish Creek Provincial Park, East End, SE

Route 27: North Calgary, NW/NE
Route 28: Peak to Peak (Nose Hill Park/Broadcast Hill), NW/SW/NE
Route 29: River Valley Ride, NW/SW/NE/SE
Route 30: Glenmore Reservoir/Elbow River, SW
Route 31: Irrigation Canal to Chestermere, SE
Route 32: South Calgary, SW/SE
Route 33: Tour de Calgary Figure Eight, NE/NW/SE/SW

Beginner Rides (mostly flat on quiet paths)
Route 1: Baker Park/Bowness Park, NW
Route 2 : Edgemont Park Ravines, NW
Route 3: Airport, NE
Route 4: Confederation Park, NW
Route 5: Elliston Regional Park, SE
Route 6: Griffith Woods, SW
Route 9: Nose Hill Park (Flat), NW
Route 13: Nose Creek/West Nose Creek Park, NE
Route 18: Inglewood Bird Sanctuary/Carburn Park, SE
Route 21: Glenmore Reservoir/Fish Creek Provincial Park, SW
Route 24: Fish Creek Provincial Park, West End, SW
Route 26: Fish Creek Provincial Park, East End, SE
Route 31: Irrigation Canal to Chestermere, SE

After-Work Rides (route that take 1–2 hours)
Route 3: Airport, NE
Route 7: Bowmont Park/Scenic Acres Ravines, NW
Route 8: West Nose Creek Park/Nose Hill Park, NW
Route 9: Nose Hill Park (Flat), NW
Route 10: Nose Hill Park (Hilly), NW
Route 11: Bowness/Bowmont Park, NW
Route 12: Confederation Park–Nose Hill Park, NW
Route 13: Nose Creek/West Nose Creek Park, NE
Route 14: Patterson Heights/Strathcona/Edworthy Park, SW
Route 15: Wildwood/Bridgeland, SW/NW
Route 16: Sunnyside/Confederation Park/Parkdale, NW
Route 17: Inglewood/Mount Royal/Scotsman's Hill, SE/SW
Route 18: Inglewood Bird Sanctuary/Carburn Park, SE
Route 20: Mount Royal/River Valley/Knob Hill, SW
Route 21: Glenmore Reservoir/Fish Creek Provincial Park, SW
Route 22: Glenmore Reservoir, SW

Route 23: Carburn Park/Douglasdale/Fish Creek Provincial Park, SE
Route 24: Fish Creek Provincial Park, West End, SW
Route 25: Fish Creek Provincial Park/McKenzie/Douglasdale, SE
Route 26: Fish Creek Provincial Park, East End, SE
Route 31: Irrigation Canal to Chestermere, SE

Challenging Rides (hilly or long or both)

Route 8: West Nose Creek Park/Nose Hill Park, NW
Route 12: Confederation Park/Nose Hill Park, NW
Route 14: Patterson Heights/Strathcona/Edworthy Park, SW
Route 15: Wildwood/Bridgeland, SW/NW
Route 19: Garrison Woods/Mount Royal/Glenmore Reservoir, SW
Route 20: Mount Royal/River Valley/Knob Hill, SW
Route 27: North Calgary, NW/NE
Route 28: Peak to Peak (Nose Hill Park/Broadcast Hill), NW/SW/NE
Route 29: River Valley Ride, NW/SW/NE/SE
Route 30: Glenmore Reservoir/Elbow River, SW
Route 32: South Calgary, SW/SE
Route 33: Tour de Calgary Figure Eight, NE/NW/SE/SW

Soak up the view of Bridgeland and downtown Calgary from atop Tom Campbell's Hill.

Nature Rides (much of the route travels through parks and green spaces)

Route 1: Baker Park/Bowness Park, NW
Route 2: Edgemont Park Ravines, NW
Route 4: Confederation Park, NW
Route 5: Elliston Regional Park, SE
Route 6: Griffith Woods, SW
Route 7: Bowmont Park/Scenic Acres Ravines, NW
Route 8: West Nose Creek Park/Nose Hill Park, NW
Route 9: Nose Hill Park (Flat), NW
Route 10: Nose Hill Park (Hilly), NW
Route 11: Bowness/Bowmont Park, NW
Route 12: Confederation Park–Nose Hill Park, NW
Route 13: Nose Creek/West Nose Creek Park, NE
Route 14: Patterson Heights/Strathcona/Edworthy Park, SW
Route 17: Inglewood/Mount Royal/Scotsman's Hill, SE/SW
Route 18: Inglewood Bird Sanctuary/Carburn Park, SE
Route 19: Garrison Woods/Mount Royal/Glenmore Reservoir, SW
Route 21: Glenmore Reservoir/Fish Creek Provincial Park, SW
Route 22: Glenmore Reservoir, SW
Route 23: Carburn Park/Douglasdale/Fish Creek Provincial Park, SE
Route 24: Fish Creek Provincial Park, West End, SW
Route 25: Fish Creek Provincial Park/McKenzie/Douglasdale, SE
Route 26: Fish Creek Provincial Park, East End, SE
Route 30: Glenmore Reservoir/Elbow River, SW
Route 32: South Calgary, SW/SE
Route 33: Tour de Calgary Figure Eight, NE/NW/SE/SW

Non-Stop Rides (mostly on bike paths with very few stops at intersections)

Route 1: Baker Park/Bowness Park, NW
Route 2: Edgemont Park Ravines, NW
Route 3: Airport, NE
Route 4: Confederation Park, NW
Route 5: Elliston Regional Park, SE
Route 6: Griffith Woods, SW
Route 9: Nose Hill Park (Flat), NW
Route 10: Nose Hill Park (Hilly), NW
Route 13: Nose Creek/West Nose Creek Park, NE
Route 15: Wildwood/Bridgeland, SW/NW
Route 18: Inglewood Bird Sanctuary/Carburn Park, SE
Route 22: Glenmore Reservoir, SW

Route 23: Carburn Park/Douglasdale/Fish Creek Provincial Park, SE
Route 24: Fish Creek Provincial Park, West End, SW
Route 25: Fish Creek Provincial Park/McKenzie/Douglasdale, SE
Route 26: Fish Creek Provincial Park, East End, SE
Route 27: North Calgary, NW/NE
Route 29: River Valley Ride, NW/SW/NE/SE
Route 30: Glenmore Reservoir/Elbow River, SW
Route 31: Irrigation Canal to Chestermere, SE
Route 32: South Calgary, SW/SE
Route 33: Tour de Calgary Figure Eight, NE/NW/SE/SW

Foodie Rides (coffee shops, ice cream or lunch stops are en route)
Route 1: Baker Park/Bowness Park, NW
Route 3: Airport, NE
Route 5: Elliston Regional Park, SE
Route 8: West Nose Creek Park/Nose Hill Park, NW
Route 11: Bowness/Bowmont Park, NW
Route 12: Confederation Park/Nose Hill Park, NW
Route 13: Nose Creek/West Nose Creek Park, NE

This South Calgary mini-park near Marda Loop sports dramatic hues in autumn.

Route 14: Patterson Heights/Strathcona/Edworthy Park, SW
Route 15: Wildwood/Bridgeland, SW/NW
Route 16: Sunnyside/Confederation Park/Parkdale, NW
Route 17: Inglewood/Mount Royal/Scotsman's Hill, SE/SW
Route 19: Garrison Woods/Mount Royal/Glenmore Reservoir, SW
Route 20: Mount Royal/River Valley/Knob Hill, SW
Route 21: Glenmore Reservoir/Fish Creek Provincial Park, SW
Route 22: Glenmore Reservoir, SW
Route 23: Carburn Park/Douglasdale/Fish Creek Provincial Park, SE
Route 25: Fish Creek Provincial Park/McKenzie/Douglasdale, SE
Route 26: Fish Creek Provincial Park, East End, SE
Route 27: North Calgary, NW/NE
Route 28: Peak to Peak (Nose Hill Park/Broadcast Hill), NW/SW/NE
Route 29: River Valley Ride, NW/SW/NE/SE
Route 30: Glenmore Reservoir/Elbow River, SW
Route 32: South Calgary, SW/SE
Route 33: Tour de Calgary Figure Eight, NE/NW/SE/SW

Neighbourhood Home-and-Garden Rides

Route 7: Bowmont Park/Scenic Acres Ravines, NW
Route 11: Bowness/Bowmont Park, NW
Route 14: Patterson Heights/Strathcona/Edworthy Park, SW
Route 15: Wildwood/Bridgeland, SW/NW
Route 16: Sunnyside/Confederation Park/Parkdale, NW
Route 17: Inglewood/Mount Royal/Scotsman's Hill, SE/SW
Route 19: Garrison Woods/Mount Royal/Glenmore Reservoir, SW
Route 20: Mount Royal/River Valley/Knob Hill, SW
Route 21: Glenmore Reservoir/Fish Creek Provincial Park, SW

Fall Colours Rides

Route 1: Baker Park/Bowness Park, NW
Route 4: Confederation Park, NW
Route 7: Bowmont Park/Scenic Acres Ravines, NW
Route 9: Nose Hill Park (Flat), NW
Route 10: Nose Hill Park (Hilly), NW
Route 11: Bowness/Bowmont Park, NW
Route 12: Confederation Park/Nose Hill Park, NW
Route 15: Wildwood/Bridgeland, SW/NW
Route 16: Sunnyside/Confederation Park/Parkdale, NW
Route 17: Inglewood/Mount Royal/Scotsman's Hill, SE/SW

Route 19: Garrison Woods/Mount Royal/Glenmore Reservoir, SW
Route 20: Mount Royal/River Valley/Knob Hill, SW
Route 21: Glenmore Reservoir/Fish Creek Provincial Park, SW
Route 22: Glenmore Reservoir, SW
Route 23: Carburn Park/Douglasdale/Fish Creek Provincial Park, SE
Route 24: Fish Creek Provincial Park, West End, SW
Route 25: Fish Creek Provincial Park/McKenzie/Douglasdale, SE
Route 26: Fish Creek Provincial Park, East End, SE
Route 30: Glenmore Reservoir/Elbow River, SW
Route 32: South Calgary, SW/SE
Route 33: Tour de Calgary Figure Eight, NE/NW/SE/SW

Rollerblade Routes (a rollerblade route is suggested)
Route 1: Baker Park/Bowness Park, NW
Route 2 : Edgemont Park Ravines, NW
Route 3: Airport, NE
Route 4: Confederation Park, NW
Route 5: Elliston Regional Park, SE
Route 6: Griffith Woods, SW

A peaceful autumn day in the west end of Fish Creek Provincial Park.

Route 8: West Nose Creek Park/Nose Hill Park, NW
Route 11: Bowness/Bowmont Park, NW
Route 12: Confederation Park–Nose Hill Park, NW
Route 13: Nose Creek/West Nose Creek Park, NE
Route 15: Wildwood/Bridgeland, SW/NW
Route 17: Inglewood/Mount Royal/Scotsman's Hill, SE/SW
Route 18: Inglewood Bird Sanctuary/Carburn Park, SE
Route 19: Garrison Woods/Mount Royal/Glenmore Reservoir, SW
Route 20: Mount Royal/River Valley/Knob Hill, SW
Route 21: Glenmore Reservoir/Fish Creek Provincial Park, SW
Route 22: Glenmore Reservoir, SW
Route 23: Carburn Park/Douglasdale/Fish Creek Provincial Park, SE
Route 25: Fish Creek Provincial Park/McKenzie/Douglasdale, SE
Route 30: Glenmore Reservoir/Elbow River, SW
Route 31: Irrigation Canal to Chestermere, SE

Urban Adventure Rides (the route passes by funky shopping and people-watching and café districts)
Route 5: Elliston Regional Park, SE
Route 16: Sunnyside/Confederation Park/Parkdale, NW
Route 17: Inglewood/Mount Royal/Scotsman's Hill, SE/SW
Route 20: Mount Royal/River Valley/Knob Hill, SW
Route 33: Tour de Calgary Figure Eight, NE/NW/SE/SW

Index

(the numbers listed in parentheses are the bike route numbers)

ABOUT FIFTH HOUSE

FIFTH HOUSE PUBLISHERS, a Fitzhenry & Whiteside company, is a proudly western- Canadian press. Our publishing specialty is non-fiction as we believe that every community must possess a positive understanding of its worth and place if it is to remain vital and progressive. Fifth House is committed to "bringing the West to the rest" by publishing approximately twenty books a year about the land and people who make this region unique. Our books are selected for their quality, saleability, and contribution to the understanding of western-Canadian (and Canadian) history, culture, and environment.

Look for the following Fifth House titles at your local bookstore:

Calgary's Best Hikes and Walks by Lori Beattie

Calgary's Historic Union Cemetery: A Walking Guide by Harry M. Sanders

The Canadian Rockies Guide to Wildlife Watching by Michael Kerr

A Hiker's Guide to Art of the Canadian Rockies by Lisa Christensen

A Hiker's Guide to the Rocky Mountain Art of Lawren Harris by Lisa Christensen

The Lake O'Hara Art of J. E. H. Macdonald and Hiker's Guide by Lisa Christensen

When Do You Let the Animals Out? A Field Guide to Rocky Mountain Humour by Michael Kerr